Dedicated to my loving husband Martin Clayton and loving parents who supported me in my walk with God and evangelism.

CONTENTS

SCRIPTURE REFERENCES

Introduction...Hi my name is Annabel. I don't profess to be a great writer or scholar but I wrote this book the best way I could. I have believed in Jesus most of my life since childhood my first time sharing the gospel I remember was age 5 telling the little girl next door that Jesus loved her and did she have him in her heart. When I ran home to tell my grandparents that she didn't have Jesus in her heart I felt great sorrow & this started a seed in me to share Jesus with

King James Bible
Cry aloud, spare not, lift up
thy voice like a trumpet, and
shew my people their
transgression, and the house

everyone I could. No matter what age you are or where you have come from Jesus wants you to be His disciple and take the good news of eternal life He offers to all you can. John 3:16 "For God so loved the world that He gave His only begotten Son that whosoever believes in Him should not perish but have everlasting life."

Who wouldn't want everlasting life?

Motorcycle evangelism ☺

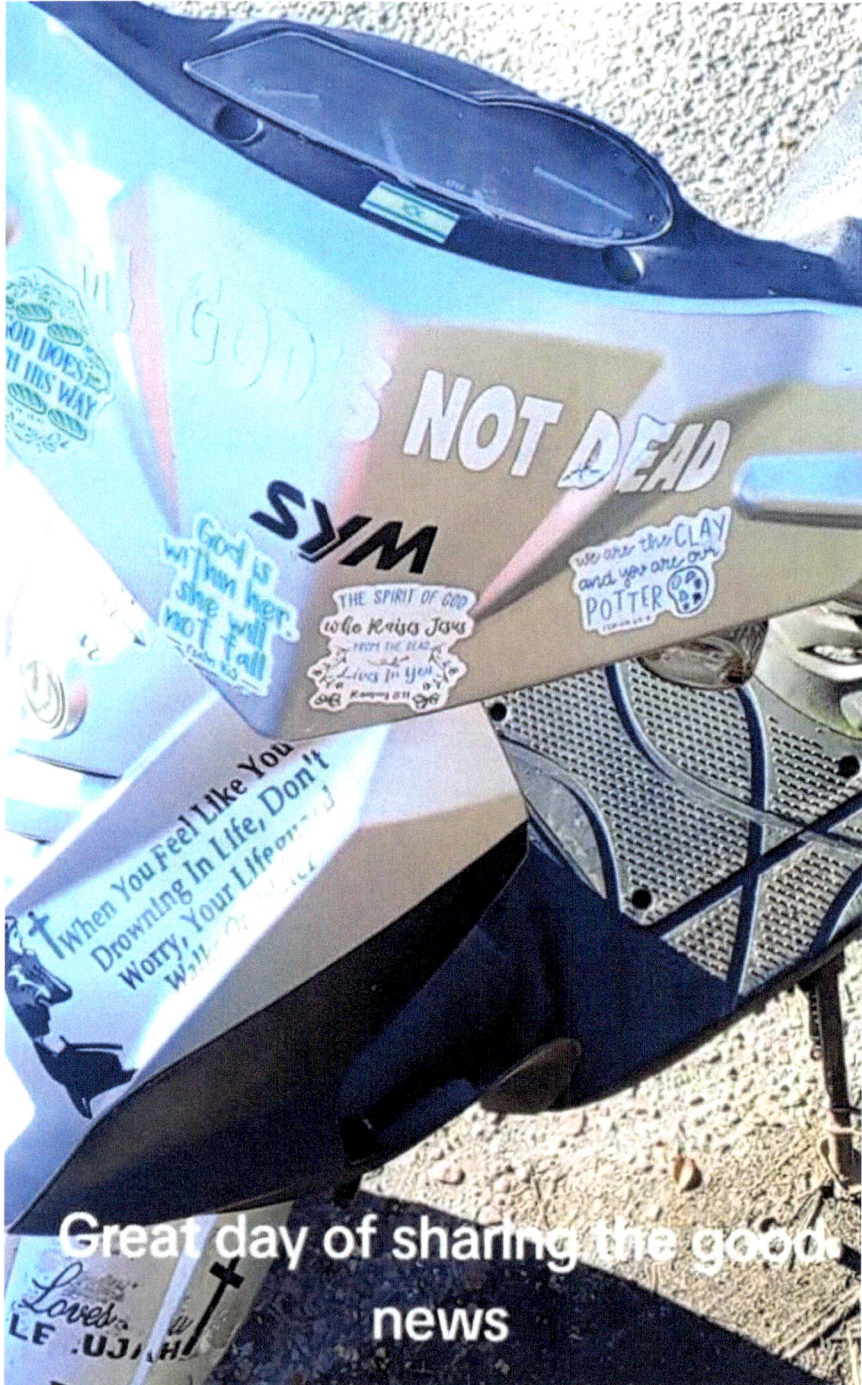

THE DREAM BEGAN

Over the years I would share my faith at school and with friends and people I met randomly while out and about walking my dog. Many people would smile at me and say thank you that's sweet to hear Jesus loves me but I never knew if they believed in their hearts or not and looking back I remember feeling great joy every time I had a positive reply.

Jesus was and is my best friend and why wouldn't I want the world to know Him and the amazing place called heaven we can go to when we die.

At big school I was called a Bible basher and labelled by my school teachers often as trouble as I would disrupt the class when they went against the Bible saying lies like we evolved or that all religions were good. This made me unpopular and often the butt of many jokes. I felt isolated and would often go home in tears and hide away in my room eating for comfort. I really wanted to share about Jesus but not many of the people I knew supported me or made me feel loved so I never knew how to follow the desire I had inside to tell the world about my saviour.

 As I grew up I made some friends mainly non believers and fell into sin. God never left me and I always spoke about him even when I was in night clubs and danced to songs thinking of God which sounds bizarre but true as even words of songs turned into Christian ones in my mind. Looking back I guess this was because I had the Holy Spirit living in me as I had accepted Jesus as my saviour early on.

Bible says when we believe that Jesus being God died and rose again three days later for our lifetime of sins we are sealed by the Holy Spirit who is in fact God living in us.

The Bible came alive to me more and more but mostly after I repented of my sinful lifestyle and came back to seeking God and reading His word.

Scriptures I had learned as a child came alive and God became a real living God to me again and not just a thought or idea.

Time went on and I got baptized to show I was changed. Many people came to my baptism and it was so encouraging to me and my family to see what God was doing in my life.

The evangelist in me was awakened and I wanted to go and share the gospel to people again on a changed level which I now understand sin better and why it was so important again that Jesus took it all for us on the cross.

What more could I do for God?. Years went by again and we got mobile phones and Facebook opened up a great opportunity to share about Jesus to my friends from years past and so I started to write about Him daily and share memes and bible scriptures.

This was the beginning of a powerful journey with God and so many opportunities opened up for me.

God had started to piece together the work that had begun in me.

Years passed and in all my jobs I got to share about Jesus to the people I worked with I noticed many had a different Jesus to me and others no faith at all. I researched more about their different beliefs in order to help me understand them better to share the true Jesus and gospel to them.

This sparked my passion for talking to cults and really wanted to see them saved by the real Jesus and the Holy Spirit taught me well as I studied the scriptures.

Marriage happened and my Christian husband Martin encouraged me every step of the way to build on my faith and support me in prayer and protection as I went out on my moped to take the gospel to the false religions leaving gospel tracts through their doors.

Little did we know that our wedding song "we've only just begun" would be so poignant to what was ahead.

This all became possible because I started a job in home care and realized I could share about Jesus by wearing clothes with Jesus written on and bags with my work stuff in. Even in the traffic on my moped people could read the name of Jesus and even read the gospel on my top especially at traffic lights when stopped.

On days when I was tired God would send encouragement when people in the petrol station would say" love your top, Jesus is amazing"

My preaching gear caught the attention of many including families of people I cared for enquiring as to where I got my Jesus hoodies giving me the opportunity to tell them that Jesus loves them and there is a heaven.

I was so excited and driven to share the good news but sadly got injured in a motorcycle crash breaking my right knee and causing me to give up on home care as my confidence was effected. It's times like that that God gives to reflect and grow in knowledge, prayer, patience. As soon as I was healed up I couldn't wait to get out again with every physio appointment I could see the hope of returning to work for the Lord nearer and nearer.

It's so strange to say but yet again worldly songs turned into hope when I heard them doing my stretches at the hospital" I believe" by happy clappers made me smile and give me hope as I yet again turned it into a song about my faith and hope but now I was right with the Lord.

Going door to door with gospel tracts was now possible due to recovery and I found several sites online with great ideas including gospel coins which could be given as gifts or left in random places.

My desire and direction opened up more and I made a YouTube channel called 'Believer in the everlasting life" and a tiktok which has proven challenging but amazing for evangelism one on one and reaching more people.

(I speak more on this later in the book)

My job situation changed and sadly we lost Martin's step dad and his dad all in a very short space of time not knowing what was approaching and the sudden loss of my mother brought things to a holt while we went through the funerals and grieving began.

The Bible encouraged us all so much as we listen to the scriptures again about God comforting us in these times and how He is near to the broken hearted.

All this life experience was preparing my heart for a deeper evangelism and closer walk with Jesus.

Doors began to open I had never dreamed of and this was the start of the wonderful adventure for Jesus and fulfilling of His will in our life.

I have learned that like a father will accept a childs picture of something even though he may not know what it is he does so as he loves his child.

To God just do your best and He will take care of the rest.

Since being a street evangelist I have come across many challenges some of which may surprise you.

From the beginning I knew I wanted to reach more people with the gospel and sharing online was fruitful. My YouTube channel and tiktok alone were giving me many subscribers and people who were hearing the true gospel. Through those platforms I could reach cults too and share with them scriptures to prove Jesus was God making them question their beliefs about God and so seeds of truth in their hearts.

The greatest obstacle to the none believer is themselves and if they are at least engaging in conversation with you you can get some truth bombs in there leaving them wondering and seeking more information.

An angry atheist is a good start as they are talking to you and can even lead other people to engage in the conversation this reaching more people.

Many times people would tag their friends in my posts saying "look at this one" or hey bro listen to this". It has always baffled me as to how I am a bruh or a bro but it seems to be the given name for reference to me so I embrace it now with a smiley face emoji.

I had a lightbulb moment and thought I can go on the train to take the gospel for to door to areas that I couldn't go to on my moped so I began going out once a week or twice a month on the train with one of my dogs for support and tracting the houses in different locations.

It became a real thrill to see how many I had done in one trip often 600 tracts and the gospel coins were handy for leaving in parks on trains and local bus stops. I prayed after each trip and asked Christian friends to also pray for all who would read my tracts.

Working as well a two day a week job gave me the spare time I needed and I was also meeting new believers on line who I could share my adventures with and pray for theirs.

When I say God moves He really does.

One story was of a man I met in a wheelchair he was an ex street preacher and he came out of the blue with his little dog in tow and just at the right moment.

I had had an encounter with a woman as I was putting tracts out who said Jesus only died for the Jews and I was a bit shaken and discouraged and along he came.

God knows how to send us help in times of trouble or discouragement and through meeting this man named Shane he gave me great directions of where to take the rest of my tracts and that day I went home singing and praise God for His never ending help.

When were obedient God really does work in us.

So let's dig into how I got to evangelize on the streets. Never in my wildest dreams did I think I could have the confidence to speak aloud to people I didn't know let alone in a public place or open air environment. The fear of man bringeth a snare: but whoso putteth his trust in the LORD shall be safe. Proverbs 29:25 This was the main scripture that helped me to get out there and just do it a the advert says.

I met a lovely Christian lady who helped me build my confidence and we went out to share about Jesus in the local towns giving away free bibles and other items to do with God. We got well known and people asked for prayer and took the free Bibles and items often offering donations to help buy more stock. God was at work.

Out of all my years of evangelizing and speaking to people about Jesus these days were feeling more exciting and I could see fruit coming from my labor in reality.

Should woman street evangelise is often the question asked to us and are we even allowed to be on the streets at all doing God's work?

Well let's see what the Bible says.

So the first woman to see Jesus resurrection and share the news was Mary Magdalene. John 20:18 Mary Magdalene came and told the disciples that she had seen the Lord, and that he had spoken these things unto her.

Later in the Bible we see Priscilla alongside he husband taught and evangelised even explaining scriptures to Apollos. Jesus never put woman down for wanting to bring the good news He offers or for speaking to men about Jesus and the confusion comes when scriptures are muddled up with woman not preaching in churches.

Acts 2:18 And on my servants and on my handmaidens I will pour out in those days of my Spirit; and they shall prophesy:

Deborah was used by God as a prophet and a judge and a deliverer in Israel. Check out Judges 4:4-10.

.

The streets and towns are not the Churches but the highways and byways the Bible speaks about so to any woman out there who feel they can't go out and share the gospel let me reassure you by the words of the Bible that you can do it!

The group I was in went in different directions and I was wondering how I could still reach the lost for Jesus and didn't know where to start.

A Christian friend of mine introduced me to a church and I met a lady there who wanted to go and speak about Jesus in towns so we arranged to meet up.

The first time we did we got told to move on by a cafe owner saying that the gospel was keeping people away from his business.

The devil of course at work as usual to try to discourage us but it didn't and we just moved on even in the rain we kept speaking aloud the gospel and handed out many tracts that day. Both of us now were convinced that God had a plan ahead for us so we decided to do the street evangelism once a week changing towns and then later buying a table to put out free items on.

I have listed in the book great places to get stock from for your evangelising ideas.

People wanted prayer and one on ones with cults even became possible as they approached us we could tell them the real gospel.

And there are also many other things which Jesus did, the which, if they should be written every one, I suppose that even the world itself could not contain the books that should be written. Amen. John 21:25

The Bible says that Jesus did so many things that even the books of the bible can't hold them and I feel like this that God did so much through just one and a half years of being on the streets that I couldn't write a book big enough.

This is my testimony

I met Annabel through a friend who knew I had the desire to go in the streets to evangelize and so we met ; it was good to meet another Christian who had the same strong desire to tell the Good News to people ; I was not very experienced but Annabel helped me with confidence and all the technical bits . I feel very happy when I do what the Lord has commanded us to do ; preach the Gospel to all people as God wants no one to perish but have eternal life and wants to give us life in its fullness . Jesus came to destroy the works of the evil one and now He is asking us to be his hands and feet on earth to show people He is the only way to God and fill our lives with peace and joy and all the fruit of the Spirit . Bijou

It's been my pleasure to share the gospel with Bijou and other Christians who I have not named in this book but there are many who serve God faithfully. Annabel

A perfect place to share about Jesus and sing some praises songs to our God

TIPS AND IDEAS FOR EVANGELISM

There are many ways to share the gospel even from your own sofa.

Below are some examples I have shared the gospel.

1) Leave tracts in library books, through doors, shops in general on shelves and hand them to people at bus stops or out and about saying thought you may like to know or other words to that effect.

2) Online. Start a YouTube channel and do videos about the Bible sharing evidence for God and the Bible being true along with helpful advice on where you can get free gospel tracts and other resources.

3) One on ones with unsaved family, neighbours, people you meet at work etc giving a tract to them or sowing some questions like " do you think there is a heaven? "Or other questions to that effect.

4) Writing letters to near by places about salvation including in there gospel tracts so to businesses etc. you don't need to add your personal info to this.

5) I fly a flag out of my window saying Jesus, the way, the truth and the life so people see the gospel that way when they walk by or you can stick up a laminated poster on your gate or on your door saying the gospel. I have stuck up how to become a Christian sign up in my gate.

6) Street evangelising. Find a church that has an evangelising group and join it or look into it other ways like at a Christian book shop where they may be asking for people to join their team. Also you could start your own evangelism team.

6.5) You can also buy Jesus loves you trolley token to leave in trolley for someone to find

7) Leave out gospel coins on benches and bus stops etc where people will be or parks where people take their children. They are lovely items to have and give the gospel in a gift form.

8) Clothing with the gospel on it. Clothes that tell you to trust Jesus for salvation or even with the name of Jesus on alone are great ways to share about God. Below I have listed where you can find these items.

9) Going on the train is a great way of reaching other towns and even speak in to people on the transport and leaving out tracts or coins in the seating areas.

10) Once in another town by train you can then spend a few hours going door to door with tracts, visiting the local parks and leaving gospel coins and even sticking stickers about that are easy to remove saying Jesus loves you on them.

11) Public toilets are a great place to pop up a little gospel sticker or leave a gospel coin. The toilet facilities cleaner will take to look at if left and other people popping through. A sticker placed on back of toilet door can be read easily by people sitting on loo and if an easy to remove one this is better.

- Gospel coins can be purchased at Living Waters Europe and Time for truth ministries(John Davis) along with other gospel tracts.

- FREE gospel tracts can be found at NEEDGOD.NET and you only need pay for the postage.

- One day publications is great for evidence books on why the bible is true
AliExpress is a site that sells all sorts of items and on there you can buy to give away Wrist bands, bookmarks, pens about Jesus and stickers etc.

- Christian clothing can be bought on AliExpress too like hoodies and t shirts again always check the wording first. Preaching Gear in America sell good clothing items including hats, banners and other preaching items so if you can afford that good to have a look. The hoodies are excellent.

- Also Ebay and Amazon sell Christian clothing just remember to check the wording.

- It's so important to memorize Bible scriptures

Internet evangelism

Technology wow this is a double edged sword. On the one hand you can use it for amazing things and on the other so many evil things too.

It has been my experience that people use the internet to try to destroy the Christian faith as well as build it. Many sites have free range over what they say and do and the amount of lies against the bible has grown over the years as well as the amount of support for the bible.

It is very important that as Christians we stand up for Gods word and truth and this can be done on the internet in various places. Tiktok has many influencers who sadly peddle lies about the Bible and God and try to lead people away from heaven and eternity with Jesus.

It's sad because of only they knew how the devil was using them as puppets for his evil plans. The heart of man is wicked the Bible says and full of all types of evil and when allowed free reign the enemy can have a field day. I never knew just how many lies there were about till I started on social media although I have heard so many everywhere and especially on the streets.

The one who can save peoples soul is hated so much because He has an enemy and that enemy as previously said is working against those who would be saved by hearing the gospel.

Gods two greatest commandments are to love Him with all your heart, mind and strength and second to love your neighbour as yourself no commandments are greater than this.

Love is to share Jesus, love is to warn sinners of what awaits without Jesus and love is to obey Jesus. How can you serve Him in your daily life?

With internet evangelism one thing to watch out for is giving pearls to swine and getting into arguments. When you share about Jesus the truth will outweigh any lies so you already have the right stand point.

If people tag their friends in your comments you can be glad as this means more people will hear the gospel.

When sharing your faith on line you will also grow stronger in your walk with God and your faith will grow as you share the truth it helps to strengthen your own faith.

Lovely day in sunny Bournemouth handing out gospel tracts

Some of the items we give away to people on the town

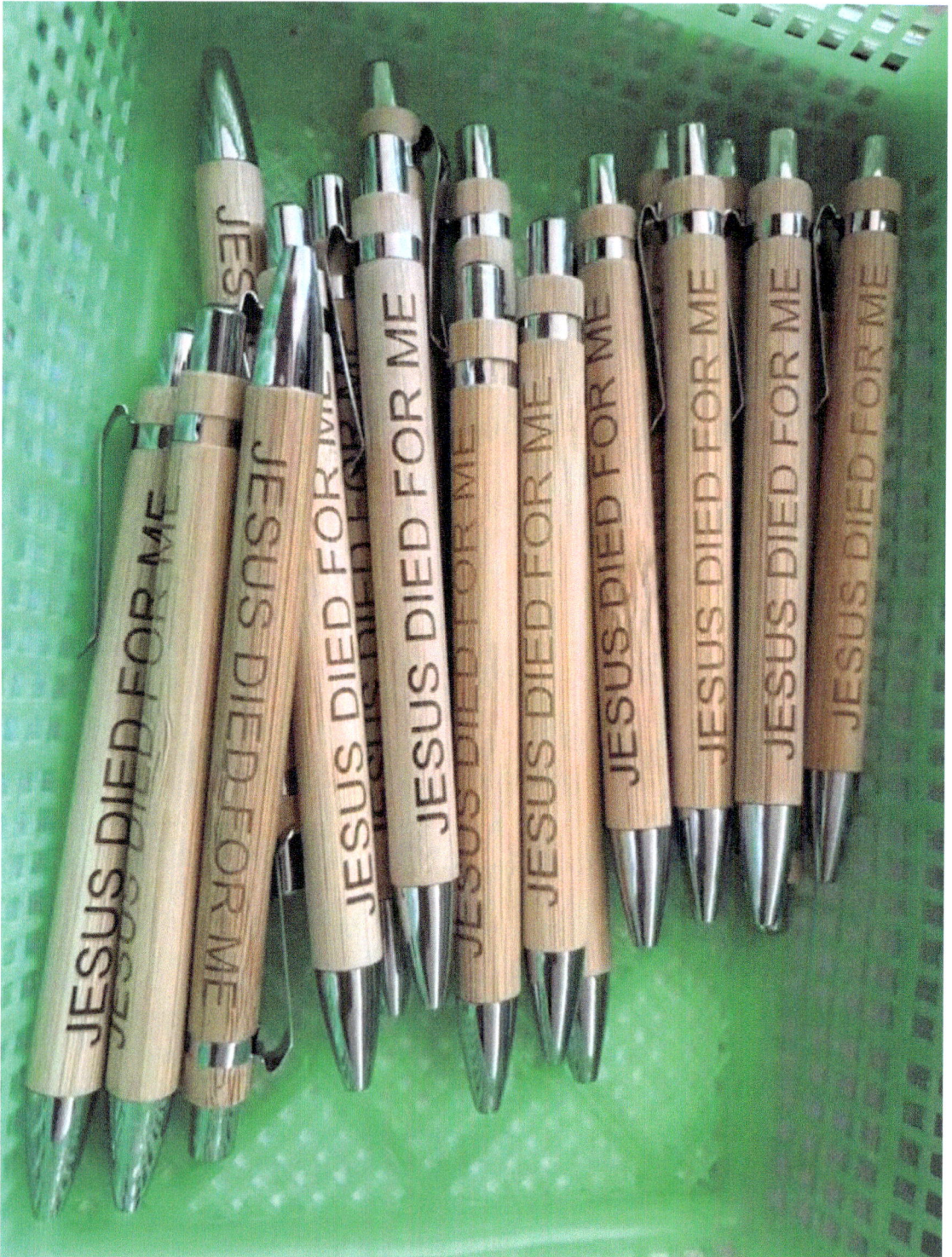

Gift bags to give away to people

ITEMS WE HAVE ON THE TABLE FOR PEOPLE..

Bibles both types easy to read and king James

Jesus loves you stickers with Bible scripture

Bible book marks and Bible scripture cards

Gospel tracts

Gospel keyrings

Christian dvds

Wrist bands about Jesus

Pens with Bible scriptures on

Gift bags about the Lord

Booklets about creation and evidence for Bible

table with free items for people to encourage them with their walk with God or seeking

It's so important to get someones identity correct or you won't know who they really are. Would you let in a stranger to your house? Neither will God.

Knowing who Jesus is is the most important for salvation as if we have another gospel or a other Jesus the bible is clear in Galatians 1:8 that you will be accursed and won't get into heaven.

When we present Jesus to the world we need to make sure we are sharing His true identity and the true gospel that saves.

Here is a list of Bible scriptures to prove Jesus is God. There are so many and these are a few great ones to help you to prove God's identity.

1) Hebrews 1 6-9 And again, when he bringeth in the firstbegotten into the world, he saith, And let all the angels of God worship him.

7 And of the angels he saith, Who maketh his angels spirits, and his ministers a flame of fire.

8 But unto the Son he saith, Thy throne, O God, is for ever and ever: a sceptre of righteousness is the sceptre of thy kingdom.

9 Thou hast loved righteousness, and hated iniquity; therefore God, even thy God, hath anointed thee with the oil of gladness above thy fellows.

1) Revelation 1:8 " I am Alpha and Omega, the beginning and the ending, saith the Lord, which is, and which was, and which is to come, the Almighty."

2) Isaiah 53 Who hath believed our report? and to whom is the arm of the Lord revealed?

2 For he shall grow up before him as a tender plant, and as a root out of a dry ground: he hath no form nor comeliness; and when we shall see him, there is no beauty that we should desire him.

3 He is despised and rejected of men; a man of sorrows, and acquainted with grief: and we hid as it were our faces from him; he was despised, and we esteemed him not.

4 Surely he hath borne our griefs, and carried our sorrows: yet we did esteem him stricken, smitten of God, and afflicted.

5 But he was wounded for our transgressions, he was bruised for our iniquities: the chastisement of our peace was upon him; and with his stripes we are healed.

6 All we like sheep have gone astray; we have turned every one to his own way; and the Lord hath laid on him the iniquity of us all.

7 He was oppressed, and he was afflicted, yet he opened not his mouth: he is brought as a lamb to the slaughter, and as a sheep before her shearers is dumb, so he openeth not his mouth.

8 He was taken from prison and from judgment: and who shall declare his generation? for he was cut off out of the land of the living: for the transgression of my people was he stricken.

9 And he made his grave with the wicked, and with the rich in his death; because he had done no violence, neither was any deceit in his mouth.

10 Yet it pleased the Lord to bruise him; he hath put him to grief: when thou shalt make his soul an offering for sin, he shall see his seed, he shall prolong his days, and the pleasure of the Lord shall prosper in his hand.

11 He shall see of the travail of his soul, and shall be satisfied: by his knowledge shall my righteous servant justify many; for he shall bear their iniquities.

12 Therefore will I divide him a portion with the great, and he shall divide the spoil with the strong; because he hath poured out his soul unto death: and he was numbered with the transgressors; and he bare the sin of many, and made intercession for the transgressors.

3) John 1 1-14

King James Version

1 In the beginning was the Word, and the Word was with God, and the Word was God.

2 The same was in the beginning with God.

3 All things were made by him; and without him was not any thing made that was made.

4 In him was life; and the life was the light of men.

5 And the light shineth in darkness; and the darkness comprehended it not.

6 There was a man sent from God, whose name was John.

7 The same came for a witness, to bear witness of the Light, that all men through him might believe.

8 He was not that Light, but was sent to bear witness of that Light.

9 That was the true Light, which lighteth every man that cometh into the world.

10 He was in the world, and the world was made by him, and the world knew him not.

11 He came unto his own, and his own received him not.

12 But as many as received him, to them gave he power to become the sons of God, even to them that believe on his name:

13 Which were born, not of blood, nor of the will of the flesh, nor of the will of man, but of God.

14 And the Word was made flesh, and dwelt among us, (and we beheld his glory, the glory as of the only begotten of the Father,) full of grace and truth.

Isaiah 9:6

King James Version

6 For unto us a child is born, unto us a son is given: and the government shall be upon his shoulder: and his name shall be called Wonderful, Counsellor, The mighty God, The everlasting Father, The Prince of Peace.

4) Titus 2:13 Looking for that blessed hope, and the glorious appearing of the great God and our Saviour Jesus Christ;

5) Colossians 2:9 For in him dwelleth all the fullness of the Godhead bodily.

6) John 8:58 Jesus said unto them, Verily, verily, I say unto you, Before Abraham was, I am.

7) Matthew 1:23 Behold, a virgin shall be with child, and shall bring forth a son, and they shall call his name Emmanuel, which being interpreted is, God with us.

8) Colossians 1:15

King James Version

15 Who is the image of the invisible God, the firstborn of every creature:

9)   Genesis 1 Verses 26 to 31. And God said, Let us make man in our image, after our likeness: and let them have dominion over the fish of the sea, and over the fowl of the air, and over the cattle, and over all the earth, and over every creeping thing that creepeth upon the earth. God is referred to here as us and our so God can be revealed in more than one person although one God.

Only God has the power to forgive sins. A created God or angel cannot forgive sins.

Without the shedding of blood there is no remission of sins the bible says. Jesus is the lamb of God who takes away the sins of the world.
Hebrews 9:22

Who he is, what he wants and Gods will. Below are some of the devils tactics to try and stop our work for the Lord.

1) Divide believers

2) Personal attacks and self hatred to the believer

3) Lists our weaknesses and uses them against us

4) Uses circumstances to make you feel inadequate for what God says you can do

5) Lies about you to others

6) Sows doubts in you about your faith or at least tries to

7) Causes friction in families

8) Tries to wear down the saints make us tired so we are less effective for Jesus

9) Lies about who God is and promises false ways to heaven

10) Exalts himself above God

11) Satan loves to twist Gods word so change the true meaning and lie about who the Holy Spirit is and says "Does the bible really say and "Did God really say and did God really write the Bible or is it just words of man"

See scriptures to describe the devil and his tactics and what we should do

Be sober, be vigilant; because your adversary the devil, as a roaring lion, walketh about, seeking whom he may devour.
1 Peter 5:8

- For we wrestle not against flesh and blood, but against principalities, against powers, against the rulers of the darkness of this world, against spiritual wickedness in high places
Ephesians 6:12

- Submit yourselves therefore to God. Resist the devil, and he will flee from you.

  James 4:7

  - Ye are of your father the devil, and the lusts of your father ye will do. He was a murderer from the beginning, and abode not in the truth, because there is no truth in him. When he speaketh a lie, he speaketh of his own: for he is a liar, and the father of it.

    John 8:44

- And the Lord said unto Satan, Behold, all that he hath is in thy power; only upon himself put not forth thine hand. So Satan went forth from the presence of the Lord.

  Job 1:12

1 John 3:8 - He that committeth sin is of the devil; for the devil sinneth from the beginning. For this purpose the Son of God was manifested, that he might destroy the works of the devil.

 2 Corinthians 11:14 - And no marvel; for Satan himself is transformed into an angel of light

James 4:7 - Submit yourselves therefore to God. Resist the devil, and he will flee from you.
John 10:10 – The thief cometh not, but for to steal, and to kill, and to destroy: I am come that they might have life, and that they might have it more abundantly.

Romans 16:20 – And the God of peace shall bruise Satan under your feet shortly. The grace of our Lord Jesus Christ be with you. Amen.

Ephesians 6:11 – Put on the whole armour of God, that ye may be able to stand against the wiles of the devil.

Revelation 12:9-12 – And the great dragon was cast out, that old serpent, called the Devil, and Satan, which deceiveth the whole world: he was cast out into the earth, and his angels were cast out with him.

Ephesians 6:12
And blood, but against principalities, against powers, against the rulers of the darkness of this world, against spiritual wickedness in high places.

2 Corinthians 4:4 – In whom the god of this world hath blinded the minds of them which believe not, lest the light of the glorious gospel of Christ, who is the image of God, should shine unto them

Matthew 16:23 – But he turned, and said unto Peter, Get thee behind me, Satan: thou art an offence unto me: for thou savourest not the things that be of God, but those that be

So from the Bible we see that the devil (Satan) was once a beautiful angel who wanted to be above God infact be God and the Lord God threw him out of heaven and a third of the angels went with him because of his pride.
His job is to deceive people away from salvation and to lie as the bible calls him the father of lies.

As our Adversary:
Job:
Satan appears before God in the Book of Job, questioning Job's piety and requesting permission to test his faith.
Zechariah:
In Zechariah 3:1-2, Satan is depicted as an accuser in a heavenly court, standing before the angel of the Lord to accuse Joshua the high priest.
1 Chronicles:
In 1 Chronicles 21:1, Satan incites King David to take a census of Israel, which is later seen as a sin.
2. Symbolic References:

Serpent in Genesis:

While not explicitly named as Satan, the serpent in the Garden of Eden is often identified as Satan due to its role in tempting Adam and Eve.
Isaiah 14 and Ezekiel 28:
These passages contain symbolic language describing the fall of a king of Babylon (Isaiah) and a king of Tyre (Ezekiel) which are sometimes interpreted as alluding to the fall of Satan from heaven.

Other religions who say otherwise to the description in bible are deceived by the devil. We should always come back to God's original word to see what is true.
Satan lies about Jesus and who He is to keep people out of heaven. If he can get people trusting in a false Jesus then there is no power of salvation for them.
The true Jesus alone can save us and deceptions are many and the devil is at work.

John 3:16 For God so loved the world that He gave His only begotten Son that whosoever believes in Him shall NOT perish but have everlasting life.

Neither is there salvation in any other, for there is no other name under heaven given among men whereby we must be saved. "Acts 4:12

Romans 10:9 That if thou shalt confess with thy mouth the Lord Jesus, and shalt believe in thine heart that God hath raised him from the dead, thou shalt be saved.

A false religion is a set of beliefs that do not line up with the word of God. The Bible warned that many deceptions would come and the Israelites followed false gods and we see false gods being worshipped all over the world.

Jesus said the way to life is narrow and few find it.

Matthew 7:13-14

King James Version

13 Enter ye in at the strait gate: for wide is the gate, and broad is the way, that leadeth to destruction, and many there be which go in thereat:

14 Because strait is the gate, and narrow is the way, which leadeth unto life, and few there be that find it.

In this chapter we will look at the many false ways to heaven and why they are false and some resources and sites to further inform on how we can help people caught in such deceptions.

God wish that no man should perish but all come to the knowledge of repentance.

Lord is not slack concerning his promise, as some men count slackness; but is longsuffering to us-ward, not willing that any should perish, but that all should come to repentance. 2 Peter 3:9

Blank page... write any notes you have here.. ☺

The devil through man made false doors. Only JESUS OF THE BIBLE will open unto you.

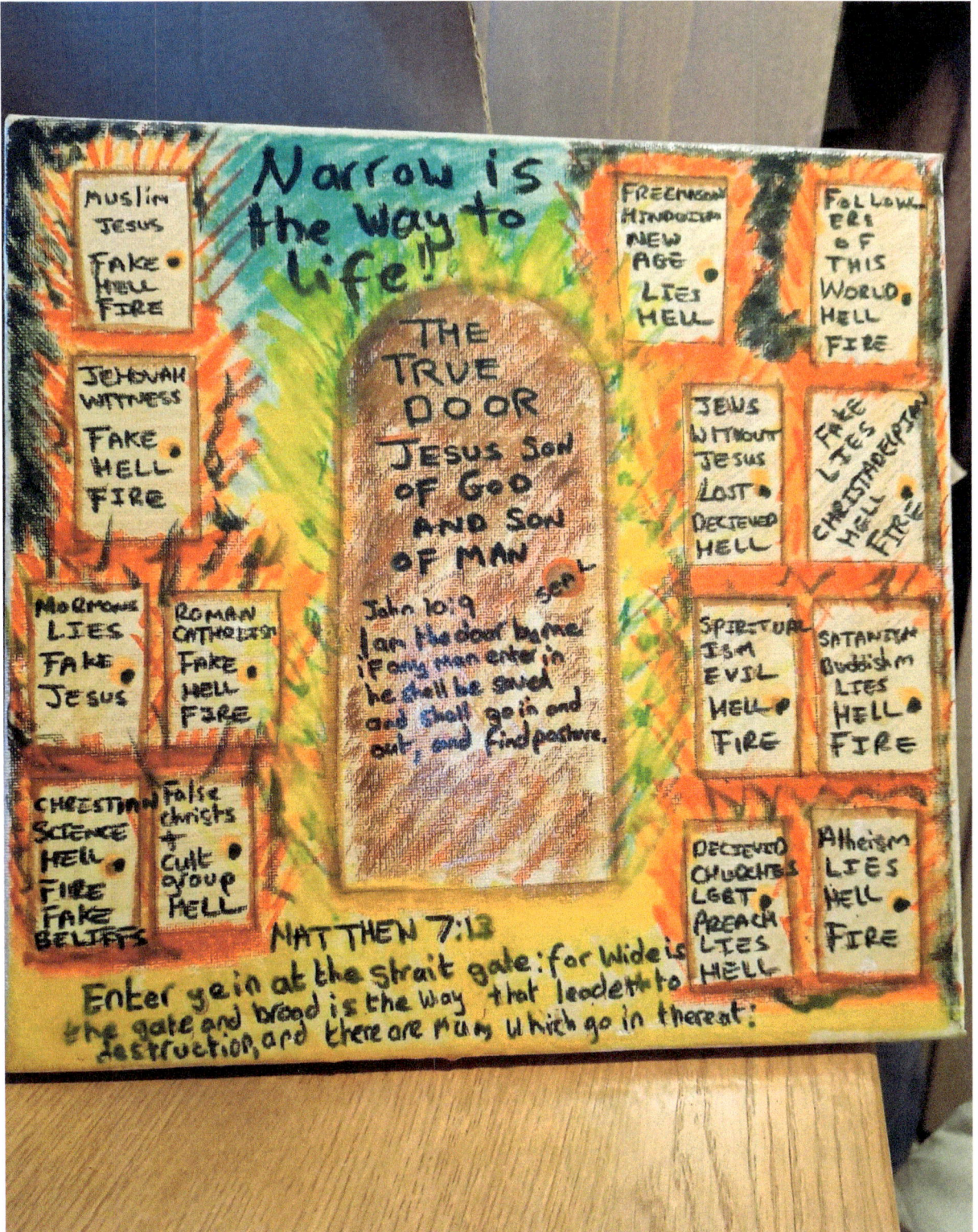

Christadelphians believe Jesus is the Son of God, but not God himself. They deny the traditional Christian doctrine of the Trinity.

Islam believes that Jesus is a prophet and not divine.

Judaism does not accept Jesus as God

Hinduism Jesus is not worshipped as God

Buddhism Jesus is not considered divine

Unitarianism rejects the trinity and says Jesus is not God

Jehovah's witnesses believe Jesus is Son of God not equal to God

Mormonism Jesus is divine but a separate being from the father

Christian science Jesus was a human but not God

Scientology Jesus is minimized in upper level teachings

Shinto no concept as Jesus as God

Baha'i faith does not accept the trinity or Jesus exclusive divinity

Sikhism Sikhs view Jesus as a revered figure, a prophet, and a holy person, but not as God.

Atheism is a religion in itself that says there is no God at all

Agnostic says there is a chance but no certainty

Roman Catholism says that Jesus is God and died for sins but you need to follow the Roman Catholic teachings to be saved

Orthodox Church believes that you need to pray to Mary and that icons are not IDOLATRY

New age you can become your own God no need for Jesus

Seventh day Adventists believe that Jesus is Michael the Archangel.

There are other cult religions out there. Test all things as the Bible says.

So you can see for the above that Satan has been busy at work deceiving many people away from Jesus true identity.

You can see from the above that Jesus is mentioned in all but not correctly.

When Jesus died and rose again it was finished all sins have been paid for and no need for further sacrifices.

The only one who gains from following these lies is the devil.

Some people who have come out of these religions are..

Mike Gendron an ex Roman Catholic his channel is on YouTube and tiktok and he can be found on Facebook.

There is a group who help people with coming out of Christian science and a book written by ex Christian science followers is available to buy called ... leaving Christian Science 10 stories of new faith in Jesus Christ by Lauren Hunter (Fellowship of Former Christian Scientists)

YouTube can show many testimonys of men and woman who have left Islam and there are some good teachers to show you the rest of what is wrong on these false religions available on line.

I recommend Brad Zockoll at the heaven tour for answers about heaven and common questions we have about the Bible. He only shares what the Bible says and is well studied in the Greek.

My prayer is that many people will see the true gospel and come to the light who is the true Jesus God who died in the flesh for all the worlds sins once.

The Bible is clear that there is no excuse for not believing in God as even the creation points to God being real.

Romans 1:20 For the invisible things of him from the creation of the world are clearly seen, being understood by the things that are made, even his eternal power and Godhead; so that they are without excuse:

Other lies about Jesus are that He is a created God, created angel, just a man.

How to do it and why. The reason why is because you reach a large amount of people and you can have some great conversations answering questions people have that people may not go into a church to ask.

How to street evangelize.

- Have a group that are united on biblical truth and have a desire to see people saved and into Gods kingdom
- Have a good pot of money available to buy Bibles and other items to give away for free
- Have a table to place items on
- Know the word of God study it and learn scriptures
- Make sure you have spare time available and transport
- Be prepared to travel out of your area
- Take food, spare money and drinks
- Plan ahead on location, time and parking if needed
- Take a Bible
- Have a we are not Jehovah's witnesses sign as it saves telling people that ask
- Check the law in the area you go to on noise audiences
- Buy a speaker of some type to project your voice through

You can buy a few types of speakers online and headsets. See which one best suits you and they normally come with all the instructions you should need. It is good to have a spare if one breaks and always have it charged up ready.

So now you have everything place have prayer time to see where God wants you to go and plan what topic you want to talk on.

God sends the right people to you and pray ahead that He will prepare the hearts to receive the gospel. When giving the gospel it's always good to back up what you say with Bible scriptures and invite people to ask questions.

It's good to ask questions and engage with your audience.

Any hecklers is a good thing as it draws people to hear the gospel.

Had this sign made as people asked if we are Jehovah's witnesses.

We are not
Jehovah's witnesses
but born again
Christians

Start off by setting up your table with all the items you want to give away and any notices or signs. Keep your belongings safe under table or behind.

Makes sure the area you choose is in a good location sheltered if possible from wind with plenty of area for it to be viewed in the flow to the side of passersby.

You can have a prepared talk or just go by leading as Gods Spirit works through you. Pray first and have some people handing out tracts and having conversations while one speaks.

It's good to advertise your table as what you have on it and that's it's FREE.

Then you can play music through. Bluetooth and sing songs about Jesus this attracts an audience and lifts up the name of Jesus bringing in an atmosphere of praise.

If anyone starts to heckle you you can either stop and answer them or one of the team can chat to them.

It's always good to set up near Jehovah's witnesses at least near by area so they can hear you sharing the truth about Jesus .

Keep a video camera going so use a phone on stand to record what you say so if any issues with anyone the video can be watched back also for your protection .

You can do this and you will get great satisfaction from seeing seeds sown and looking back at the interactions you have had.

Always take a pen and paper to make note of names to pray for or add to your phone album.

The most rewarding part is when you know that God has been at work and you have been the hands and feet He required.

Treasures in heaven and where one sows another man will reap.

Mark 15:16 And he said to them, "Go into all the world and proclaim the gospel to the whole creation.

Matthew 28:16-20

King James Version

16 Then the eleven disciples went away into Galilee, into a mountain where Jesus had appointed them.

17 And when they saw him, they worshipped him: but some doubted.

18 And Jesus came and spake unto them, saying, All power is given unto me in heaven and in earth.

19 Go ye therefore, and teach all nations, baptizing them in the name of the Father, and of the Son, and of the Holy Ghost:

20 Teaching them to observe all things whatsoever I have commanded you: and, lo, I am with you always, even unto the end of the world. Amen.

THERE IS NO GREATER FEELING THAN KNOWING YOU HAVE SOWED TRUTH ABOUT JESUS IN SOMEONES HEART AND THEY ARE ON THEIR WAY TO BE SAVED.

Wow where do I begin. God has done so much through our street evangelism and my YouTube channel it's more than I can write about but I would like to share a few true stories to show that God is at work and that you can do it too and know the joy of serving God in this way.

If you have a deep desire to do more to see people saved I pray these stories fill you with hope, passion and ideas to start you off and give you that push in the right direction you may be finding hard to start.

The cults.

During our street evangelism we have encountered many people of different faiths. I could probably write tick sheet and tick most of them off.

My first outreach in the second group which I started met with some interesting hecklers. Sometimes when you go out to street preaching you come across people of other religions before you even set up the table that you can chat to in those areas and most often it's either Jehovah's witnesses or Mormons that we find out on the streets.

Bijou and I took the table to a local town by the sea and started to sing about Jesus and we both had prepared a talk. People came to say this is great and others looked at us like we were mad but that was ok as we counted it as joy.

One song we sang was step across the line by Don Fransisco. We found a line on the concrete together stood by one side of it every time it said "you have to take a step across the line we jumped over the line. I noticed people had started to video us which is great as they most likely would share it and get the gospel message out further. Words of song include show you where to look but you got to take that step across the line meaning from unbelief to belief in Jesus.

People were happy to take items from the table and let their children take things too which delighted us as the Lord was at work and we could see this in reality knowing He was with us.

Street evangelism builds your faith in God and gives you more passion to do it again.

Many people had one on ones including a Muslim who fist pumped me when we agreed on a fact about the true God. On one day out we could hand out up to 60 or more gospel tracts and as my group grew we could hand out more.

People are looking for hope and without Jesus we are all spiritually dead in our sins. Jesus gives everlasting life to whoever believes in Him.

Showing people their need of Jesus is what evangelism is all about. All have sinned and fallen short of the glory of God and the wages of sin is death which is not just this body now but eternal separation from God in hell forever.

Showing what sin is starts the ball rolling then you can show people the good news that Jesus has paid their fine their sins crimes have been covered by Him on the cross and all they need do is agree with God they have sinned and turn to Him trusting in His finished work to save them.

Hebrews 9:22 And by the law almost all things are purged with blood, and without shedding of blood there is no remission.

The free items show that God's love is free and the desire is to encourage people to seek God and read His word the Bible.

During our outreaches to the towns we had many conversations with people and got to answer the question asked by people who were genuinely looking for the truth about God .

So many people believe that they automatically go to heaven when they die just by being a human being and dying but the bible never says that. Jesus death does not automatically save everyone. Yes Jesus died to save everyone but it's a personal choice to accept what Jesus did for you personally by taking your sins and believing that Jesus is God who died and rose again in the flesh 3 days later.

Some of the stories we hear are well if God died for my sin I can keep sinning or if God died for me then I am ok and just live my life. The fact people don't understand is that without Jesus you do not have eternal life and your spirit is dead. Jesus said you must be born again to enter heaven and this is something that we like to make sure people know when sharing the gospel.

On sunny days we have had some amazing chats with people about Jesus on raining ones a few less but still always a place to shelter where others are also.

We met a French street busker who sang with us and we sang him a song in French about Jesus. After that he took a tract from us about how to be saved and a pen.

You won't know till you go to the streets just how many different people are about. Children are very keen to take things from the table and the parents seem to then take things too so it's great when you offer a wrist band saying Jesus loves on it the smiles you get are infectious.

Sometimes we keep free things in a sweet tub and children often ask if we have any free chocolate or sweets. We haven't given that out due to the fact a child may be allergic to sugar etc and what child doesn't love a sticker?

One sad story I have heard on the streets was a young man who had lost most of his family to COVID and was so angry at God. I said to him that God loves him and didn't want sin and death in the world and that heaven would be an amazing place. After praying with him he came to realize that heaven was a place he could still go to through Jesus and if his family were saved they would meet again there.

Often people in town have been through drug abuse or alcohol abuse and need to know that God wants to help them and give them a Bible and something else like a bookmark, scripture pen, gospel coin or something they can take away with them to keep them remembering the good news of Jesus. It's also good to have phone numbers with you of any Christian organizations in your area that can help people in addictions or any type of abuse situation.

One elderly Christian lady kept showing up at our table every weekend we were there and you will see the regular people going by. It makes it so special to be recognized and then to encourage them as they also encourage you back. Praying with people is always welcome and although God doesn't always heal you can always ask Him to heal people according to his will.

Facing the ones that come up and shout is a skill. Don't argue but try to stand strong on Gods truth in what to say even offering prayer to an angry by stander can help defuse the situation. I have found that if you show kindness then it really helps along with humility to bring the conviction of Gods love to the person and sow seeds they won't forget and God can use to grow over time.

I remember one young man getting very angry at me and saying all sorts of lies about Jesus. He got right up in my face and I was just holding my ground. God

God steps in in those moments as many times people later think why was i so angry at that young lady? While handing out gospel tracts we had an older man get a rubbish bag and putting the gospel tract we gave him in it and giving it back to me saying keep your religion to which I replied "thank you I needed another rubbish bag." This made by passers laugh and lightened the atmosphere.

When God is moving in the hearts of people it often will cause emotional responses so you need to be ready for anything. Going out in 2-3 groups is ideal or more if possible.

Using the microphone seems a bit daunting at first so practice with family or other Christians before you go out and keep it charged ready for use.

Signs about Jesus are a great way to show what you are about before you even speak people walking by see the name of Jesus and it reminds them that He is God and He is worth knowing about.

HEAVEN IS JESUS. If you don't love Jesus you won't love heaven is a good one liner.

Our group grew a few people but after finding it a bit tough to manage we reduced it back down . When you have a few people all wanting to share about Jesus it needs some organization and time restrictions on each person with room for the Holy Spirit to move and questions to be asked by the public.

How to start to speak? When I started out I use to use a clip board with a prepared talk to do in town and after that I had learnt what I wanted to say I remembered old talks etc and added them into new improvised talks I had about creation or evidence outside of the Bible for God.

Your main aim is to get people thinking enough that they have questions and notice they have these questions and see how they can be answered from the bible. Seeing people get saved by the Lord the same day can happen but seed sowing is where you will find most of your work goes. Making sure you give out as many gospel tracts to as many people as possible is the goal praying that God will use the seeds and bring the increase.

There is a great feeling of boldness that comes over you when you start to speak the truth about God out loud.

Women have a place in evangelism and men also and a mixed group of men and women is great as it encourages both sexes to approach the table and engage in conversations.

Often other faiths will approach you to ask you about why your religion is the truth and it's great time to give them biblical evidence for God and why Jesus is God and why He can save you. There are available tracts to hand to people of other religions that can be easily given out due to time restraints and you know you have helped to lead them to the right way.

Never feel that you have to move on when you are in the town there are some restrictions but many will use lies to try to get you to move and guilt trips like "you are stopping people buying from my business or putting them off coming in my shop" That's not true and if someone wants something nothing will put them off going into the shops.

The devil has his guilt trippers so be aware they will be around so know the law of the area and have it in writing if need be.

"Free things about Jesus and come and find it more about your Creator" helps to show people what you are about and saying this on the microphone will reach far and wide up and down both ways of the street.

When handing out tracts make it fun too. Different tracts taylor to different types of people and needs. Some tracts are made for children and others any have a theme. When thinking about which tract to give out look at the person who is taking it and think which tract would best fit that person. There are so many different designs of tracts out there even ones for the older generation and by doing this even shuffle through some while they wait and say just looking for the one God wants me to give you or just want to get the best one for you. That makes people already feel special and cared about and more willing to read the tract once they have it.

The message is the same but the layout different. I love the easy to read bible and it can be bought on line for as little as 99p each. This Bible has lovely photography in it as well as simple passages on what Jesus did and who He is.

The NEW EASY TO READ BIBLE. Available online.

Here I have listed typical objections and questions you may get when street evangelising or one on ones and how to respond.

1) Common reply when saying about salvation is "but I have heaven on earth here now."

Reply this is temporary as the Bible says...While we look not at the things which are seen, but at the things which are not seen: for the things which are seen are temporal; but the things which are not seen are eternal. 2 Corinthians 4:18 So explain that there is two places after you die heaven or hell and we all go on somewhere after we die. Sow doubt in their mind that this is everything and you have done well.

2) "I don't believe in God or that there is God."

Response Romans 1:20 says "For the invisible things of him from the creation of the world are clearly seen, being understood by the things that are made, *even* his eternal power and Godhead; so that they are without excuse:"

You can show them the evidence for God by the creation and the fact that we all have a conscience and if God wasn't real why would it matter if we lie, stole or murdered someone. That gets the ball rolling.

Ecclesiastes 3:11 states God has "set eternity in the human heart." In every human soul is a God-given awareness that there is "something more" than this transient world.

3) How do you know your religion is the right one?

This is a common question and easily answered by showing them the reliability of Jesus and the word of God. First I explain that Jesus rose from the dead and it's recorded in history that He was seen by over 500 people at one time after this happened. There is evidence outside the bible for the bibles reliability through archaeology and historical people who wrote about him. You can ask who they know who rose from the dead?

Also Jesus said " I am the way, the truth and the life and that no man cometh to the father but by Me" So Jesus was clear that He is the only way to heaven and to being right with God.

4) "He never did anything for me"

You can point out that they are breathing, have food, clothes and family maybe a home and car and the ability to enjoy the beauty around them. God scripture for this is John 1 1-5 In the beginning was the Word, and the Word was with God, and the Word was God. The same was in the beginning with God. All things were made by him; and without him was not any thing made that was made. In him was life; and the life was the light of men.

The word is Jesus and you can point out here that He is God and by Him all things were made that we all have here and **James 1:17**

King James Version[17] Every good gift and every perfect gift is from above, and cometh down from the Father of lights, with whom is no variableness, neither shadow of turning.

So you can leave that seed of truth with them or they may want to chat more on this.

Always fun to leave out gospel coins for people to find. I went in once to collect a good to go meal and handed the man a gospel coin to which he said "I found one of these the other day in the park". I was happy to hear that and told him God must really love Him. He smiled.

PENNYS FROM HEAVEN

Jesus said Matthew 24:11 And many false prophets shall rise, and shall deceive many.

So false teachers and prophets is a sign that we are in the last days before Jesus return and we should be watching out for such people.

The Bible says 1 Thessalonians 5:21 Prove all things; hold fast that which is good

We are to test what people do and judge with righteous judgement the bible says. There is a call to judge things and test things in the bible to keep yourself away from false doctrine and things that the word of God warns us of.

People who add or change Gods word in some way or take away from it are to be marked and avoided. God is very clear on that and anyone who is teaching you false doctrine is most likely an anti Christ.

There are many who take money from vulnerable people and I have seen these guys in action on God TV channels. And it's so evil. God will not be mocked and these people should be warned of the judgement coming.

Using God for financial gain or any other reason that is abuse or manipulation is not of God.

We are to win souls to Jesus not steal from them and we should be sharing with people what will edify and strengthen them not destroy them.

You can now days Google search false teachers and you will find many but others are not so easy to see so stay in the bible and test what people say and do against the word of God.

I PRAY THAT GOD WILL DIRECT YOU ON THESE ISSUES AND GIVE YOU HIS DISCERNMENT WHICH IS SO NEEDED IN THESE LAST DAYS.

A troubling thing I have noticed is the increase in people calling themselves prophets and apostles.

A prophet isn't something you train to be but a God given gift and where does the Bible say that we have apostles now?

The old testament carried a serious consequence for false prophets.

Consequences for the False Prophet

The consequences for those who engage in false prophecy are serious. Two things happened; the death penalty prescribed in Deuteronomy and Gods divine judgment. Ezekiel 13:9 declares, "My hand will be against the prophets who see false visions and utter lying divinations. They will not belong to the council of My people or be recorded in the register of the house of Israel, nor will they enter the land of Israel. Then you will know that I am the Lord GOD."

This shows the exclusion of false prophets from the community of God's people and their separation from His promises. The false prophet's deception not only leads to personal ruin also to a loss of standing and identity within the covenant community.

Biblical Warnings Against False Prophets

The Bible consistently warns against false prophets, who claim to speak on behalf of God but lead people astray with their deceitful messages. In Deuteronomy 18:20-22, the Lord provides a clear directive: "But the prophet who presumes to speak a word in My name that I have not commanded him to speak, or who speaks in the name of other gods, that prophet must die." This severe penalty underscores the gravity of falsely claiming divine authority. Then answered Amos, and said to Amaziah, I was no prophet, neither was I a prophet's son; but I was an herdman, and a gatherer of sycomore. Amos 7:14

What was an apostle?

The word apostle means "one who is sent out." In the New Testament, there are two main usages of the word apostle. The first is in specifically referring to the twelve apostles of Jesus Christ. The second is in generically referring to other individuals who are sent out to be messengers/ambassadors of Jesus Christ.

The twelve apostles held a unique position. In referring to the New Jerusalem, Revelation 21:14 states, "The wall of the city had twelve foundations, and on them were the names of the twelve apostles of the Lamb." The twelve apostles are also referred to in Matthew 10:2; Mark 3:14; 4:10; 6:7; 9:35; 14:10, 17, 20; Luke 6:13; 9:1; 22:14; John 6:71; Acts 6:2; and 1 Corinthians 15:5. It was these twelve apostles who were the first messengers of the gospel after the death and resurrection of Jesus Christ. It was these twelve apostles who were the foundation of the church—with Jesus being the cornerstone (Ephesians 2:20).

This types of apostle are not present in the church today. The qualifications of this type of apostle were: (1) to have been a witness of the resurrected Christ (1 Corinthians 9:1), (2) to have been explicitly chosen by the Holy Spirit (Acts 9:15), and (3) to have the ability to perform signs and wonders (Acts 2:43; 2 Corinthians 12:12). The responsibility of the twelve apostles, laying the foundation of the church, would also argue for their uniqueness. Two thousand years later, we are not still working on the foundation.

Beyond the unique twelve apostles of Jesus Christ, there were also apostles in a generic sense. Barnabas is referred to as an "apostle" in Acts 13:2 and 14:14. Andronicus and Junias are possibly identified as apostles in Romans 16:7. The same Greek word usually translated "apostle" is used to refer to Titus in 2 Corinthians 8:23 and Epaphroditus in Philippians 2:25. So, there definitely seems to be room for the term apostle being used to refer to someone besides the twelve apostles of Jesus Christ. Whoever was "sent" could be called an apostle.

What exactly would be the role of an apostle outside that of the twelve apostles? That is not entirely clear. From the definition of the word, the closest thing today to an apostle, in the general sense, is a missionary. A missionary is a follower of Christ who is sent out with the specific mission of proclaiming the gospel. A missionary is an ambassador of Christ to people who have not heard the good news. To avoid confusion, it is surely best to not use the name apostle to refer to any position in the church today. The majority of times the word apostle or apostles in the New Testament refer to the twelve apostles of Jesus Christ.

There are some today who want to reinstate the position of apostle. This is a bad idea. Many times those claiming to be apostles seek authority to be an improvement on the authority of the original twelve apostles. There is absolutely no biblical evidence to support such a way of thinking for the role of apostle today. This ties in with the New Testament's warning against false apostles (2 Corinthians 11:13).

In some ways all followers of Jesus Christ are called to be apostles. We are all to be His ambassadors (Matthew 28:18-20; 2 Corinthians 5:18-20). We are called to be "ones who are sent out" (Acts 1:8). We are all to be preachers of the good news (Romans 10:15).

Inconclusion we need to really know the word of God before we make claims about ourselves to others and be faithful in sharing the true gospel so we do not get under God's Judgement in wrong doing.

1) Jesus has fulfilled 313 Bible prophecies already with more to go
2) A significant portion of biblical prophecies, estimated at 80%, are believed to have been accurately fulfilled
3) Adam did not have a belly button
4) Psalm 150 lists at least six instruments used in the joyful worship of God: the trumpet (a rams horn), harp and lyre, timbrel (tambourine), pipe and cymbals
5) Jesus will return to the Mount of Olives one day
6) B I B L E basic instructions before leaving earth
7) All the new testament was written in Greek
8) Most of the old testament was first written in Hebrew
9) Hebrew is written and read from right to left
10) The Bible is 66 books in 1
11) In some Christian numerology, the number 888 is associated with Jesus
12) Both Mary and Joseph were descendants from King David who was directly descended from Adam
13) In Jerusalem you can walk through the very tunnel cut by Hezekiah's engineers to allow a safe supply of water against an Assyrian siege
14) The pool of Siloam received water through Hezekiah's underground aqueduct from the Gihon spring
15) ## The Bible was written over 1,500 years by over 40 authors across three continents in three languages
16) There are approximately 23,214 verses in the Old Testament
17) The shortest verse is John 11:35, which simply says, "Jesus wept." The longest verse is Esther 8:9
18) The Bible was written across three continents: Asia, Africa, and Europe
19) Approximately 93 women speak in the Bible
20) Methuselah is the oldest person recorded in the Bible, living 969 years

God of surprises

There is not a day that goes by when God doesn't surprise me.

In times of distress God has been my rescuer, in times of need God has been my provider and in times of uncertainty God has been my certainty.

There was a time in my life that I cried out for a husband and 3 days later I met my husband. God allows answered prayers to look back and gain faith on the days when faith is hard to find. Through the pain of losing some of our family members all very close to each other God stayed faithful and provided for us in every way.

It is at times of trouble we reach out to God the most and in those times He never fails to supply all our needs. He is an on time God, faithful and true and every time I have found myself at the cross roads God has pulled me through in ways I couldn't have written.

I grew up struggling with eating disorders and got to know a lovely Christian lady and her group who helped me through it. The ABC group was for Anorexia, Bulimia and Compulsive eaters and I was in the gang in two categories paid up and full membership and with the goodness of God I overcame these struggles showing the kindness of God to those who call out to Him in despair.

Now the ABC stands for a better invitation one that brings hope and joy in the middle of a dark and cruel world.

A acknowledge you have sinned against God

B believe that Jesus died in your place to give you everlasting life

C confess with your mouth Jesus, believe in your heart that God raised Jesus and be saved

What hope awaits those who believe in Jesus. A place in heaven with a big feast and a huge family of people to share the joy of heaven and God's presence with where there is no more sorrow or crying and all the bad thoughts and things we have gone through will be wiped away. Revelation 21:4 And God shall wipe away all tears from their eyes; and there shall be no more death, neither sorrow, nor crying, neither shall there be any more pain: for the former things are passed away.

God is offering you Heaven not Hell! His arms are stretched out to you with love saying "Come unto Me all ye who are weary and heavy laden and I will give you rest"

This is the message we have received freely and freely we can share to others.

Who inspires you?

In the Bible there are so many amazing men and woman of God it's hard to pick someone that inspires you the most. For me it was Moses and the way he stood up to Pharaoh demanding the release of the Jews from slavery. I loved the way he stood for God and challenged the love of false gods and idol worship. Now days there is so much false god worship and IDOLATRY we need modern day strong men and woman of God to stand against these deceptions and say "let my people go!" Slavery is not always in a prison but more often one that one builds through disobeying God or being ignorant of the word of God.

In life we all need to have our mentors, people who encourage us and help propel us on to our next journey or adventure with the Lord.

People of God had there supporters who would direct and teach them as they walked with God and to share the gospel it's important to have prayer support and also companionship along the way. Never underestimate a good church.

When I first started out I wasn't in a church and I found it awkward when I was asked what church I went to as I felt guilty for not attending one. This wasn't surprising as the Bible says to keep meeting together and not be like others who don't. I had been finding it hard to find a church that I liked as with so many now teaching bad doctrine and woman vicars it made me feel to come out and be separate for a time.

Meeting Bijou she encouraged me back to church and it was a good one all the boxes ticked so now feeling strong again and obedient I could boldly say where I went. I remember Brad Zockoll saying that just because you go to a bad mechanic doesn't mean you don't take your car to another one!

Now in church I have the support and prayers to help me keep going and now can help with the church team to evangelize too. God is so good. He wants us to do what's right so will provide what's is needed we need only walk and trust and He will direct our paths as proverbs says. Proverbs 3:5-6

King James Version

5 Trust in the Lord with all thine heart; and lean not unto thine own understanding.

6 In all thy ways acknowledge him, and he shall direct thy paths.

Below are scriptures to show that salvation is not something we can earn or obtain by working for it. Salvation is totally of grace from God through believing in JESUS.

1 Peter 2:24 kjv

24 Who his own self bare our sins in his own body on the tree, that we, being dead to sins, should live unto righteousness: by whose stripes ye were healed.

1 Peter 3:18 For Christ also hath once suffered for sins, the just for the unjust, that he might bring us to God, being put to death in the flesh, but quickened by the Spirit:

2 Corinthians 5:21 For he hath made him to be sin for us, who knew no sin; that we might be made the righteousness of God in him.

Romans 6:10 For in that he died, he died unto sin once: but in that he liveth, he liveth unto God.

Hebrews 10:12 But this man, after he had offered one sacrifice for sins for ever, sat down on the right hand of God;

So we can see that salvation is all of God not of us. This is the gospel we need to present to the world. We cannot add to anything Jesus has already done.

Ephesians 2:8 For by grace are ye saved through faith; and that not of yourselves: it is the gift of God:

So many religions have made gods that ask you to work for your place in heaven but God says you can't do anything accept what I did for you in your place.

Isaiah 46:6 But we are all as an unclean thing, and all our righteousness are as filthy rags; and we all do fade as a leaf, and our iniquities, like the wind, have taken us away.

We are all born spiritually dead in sins and due to Adams sin we are all under the curse of sin and death until we are born again of God's Spirit.(the Holy Spirit)

The Bible says 1 John 5:12 He that hath the Son hath life; and he that hath not the Son of God hath not life. This is another reason why what we do is so important we are literally leading people to the truth that will give them eternal life. God does the saving and we do the seed sowing and sometimes the reaping but God gives the increase.

1 Corinthians 3:6-8 King James Version

6 I have planted, Apollos watered; but God gave the increase.

7 So then neither is he that planteth any thing, neither he that watereth; but God that giveth the increase

8 Now he that planteth and he that watereth are one: and every man shall receive his own reward according to his own labour.

God wants to reward His people. God actually wants us to use our talents and have rewards on our judgement day.

When we are saved our good works and bad works are judged not our sins which means we are able to do both good and bad works but will not be under condemnation from God.

The sin has been covered by God and the transaction was Jesus in our place so now we are serving Him unto good works.

One question I have always wondered is what are bad works and what are good works?

From what I have gleaned so far is that a good work would be sowing or reaping. A bad work may be doing something we thought God wanted but He didn't or something in our flesh not in the Holy Spirit leading.

This would be a good topic to look into and about rewards that God offers to those who serve Him. An exciting time when the believers receive their rewards in an arena like place where we cheer each other on.

Always remember to ask the question "what does the Bible say on it?" and you won't go wrong.

After speaking to Brad Zockoll on what the Bible says about works we can see better from the Greek. It is to do with the value of the work.

This is what the Greek calls good works done for God. In ancient Greek, the word agathos (ἀγαθός) primarily means "good" but can also convey meanings such as "noble," "brave," "virtuous," "capable," or "beneficial,

: Phaulos fow'-los Parts of Speech Adjective

Phaulos Definition easy,worthless,ordinary,

bad,wicked etc word for bad works in the Greek.

THE BEATITUDES

Matthew 5:3-10 KJV

3 Blessed are the poor in spirit: for theirs is the kingdom of heaven.

4 Blessed are they that mourn: for they shall be comforted.

5 Blessed are the meek: for they shall inherit the earth.

6 Blessed are they which do hunger and thirst after righteousness: for they shall be filled.

7 Blessed are the merciful: for they shall obtain mercy.

8 Blessed are the pure in heart: for they shall see God.

9 Blessed are the peacemakers: for they shall be called the children of God.

10 Blessed are they which are persecuted for righteousness' sake: for theirs is the kingdom of heaven.

who took things about Jesus

Lovely Spanish people who took things about JESUS from our table

I met Andrew Diaz Russell at a church my friend attended and he was guest speaker. He had an impressive talk about how God had looked after him through lots of time in hospital and becoming blind but for God's glory.

Many years went past and I unknowingly became friends with his dad when I was out doing home care. I had my Jesus hoodie on and started a conversation chatting about his faith in Jesus and I had no idea he was related to Andrew till many years later.

Once I found out via seeing them together on a profile picture on WhatsApp I started to ask more about Andrew and how he was etc. I had started street evangelism and Andrews dad informed me Andrew also did street evangelising.

This was such a great opportunity to ask for him to join us so Andrew agreed to come and speak about Jesus with us and help by handing out tracts. Being a blind man many people noticed and that he was giving glory to God and drew some attention including a young man who rededicated his life to Jesus and went back to church.

Andrew has been coming along with the groups I have been in for a while now and he has an amazing testimony which can be found on YouTube on my evangelism channel as well as other places.

He has written books and shares about Jesus around the world speaking other languages.

Andrew out with us in town enjoying the sunshine and evangelising alongside us

WHAT IS SIN?

According to the dictionary this is a definition of sin.

Noun

An immoral act considered to be a transgression against divine law.

"a sin in the eyes of God"

The 10 commandments show us what sin is. Sin is falling short of Gods law and his standards for Holyliness.

What are the 10 commandments?

You shall have no gods before me.

You shall not make any idols to worship.

You shall not take the Lord's name in vain.

Remember the Sabbath day and keep it holy.

Honour your father and your mother.

You shall not kill.

You shall not commit adultery.

You shall not steal.

You shall not bear false witness.

You shall not covet your neighbours goods.

Seeing this list we can all see we have broken Gods law and are guilty before Him and if God were to judge us we would all be guilty and sentenced to death....

For the wages of sin is death; but the gift of God is eternal life through Jesus Christ our Lord Romans 6:23

So sin is missing Gods mark and standard for Holy living and obedience and there is a consequence for doing so which is eternal separation from God in hell.

This is why we see how great Gods sacrifice for us was. It bridges the gap between us and God and gave us back life which without Jesus paying our fine we would be unable to make ourselves.

Sin is so evil to God that He can't have any in heaven but through Him we can be washed white as snow and fit to enter heaven through Jesus righteousness given to us as a gift.

Great news God gives good gifts and His promises are yes and amen.

If a person rejects Gods offer of redemption through Jesus His Son then the only thing left is condemnation and eternal separation from God in Gods eternal jail hell where the worm never dies and there will be weeping and gnashing of teeth.

And shall cast them into a furnace of fire: there shall be wailing and gnashing of teeth Matthew 13:42

They have chosen to pay for their own sins rather than let JESUS pay for them.

 Once you know what sin is you can be sure your sins will find you out so turn to Jesus today as salvation is today and tomorrow never promised.

REPENTANCE a word that means agree with God and change your mind also to regret your sins. A wonderful word that changes the human heart from unbelief and rebellion to submission and eternal life.

Fun fact the devil and his angels have no chance of parole but humans do. We can be SAVED.

CONCLUSION

I hope you have enjoyed reading my book and it has encouraged and helped to equip you with your evangelising goals to reach the lost.

There are so many great street evangelists out there who are great and watch for ideas but I would say don't just observe go and do. YOU CAN DO IT!

God who calls you to it will bring you through it because God doesn't call the qualified He qualifies the called.

Look back in a year from now and see how much God has used you. Set out one year to aim to evangelise. Maybe start off by telling one new person a day that Jesus loves them and died for them.

Set small goals and work up to larger ones. The more you do it the more you will love it.

Imagine getting to heaven and behind you seeing names of people you have led to salvation. What Joy there is in heaven over one sinner that repents.

Keep a diary of the things you want to do for the Lord and tick them off as you achieve them.

Learn the scriptures and you will be able to have great conversations with all sorts of people and the Holy Spirit will lead you into all truth.

The best is yet to come and know any opposition is good as it shows that you are in Gods will. The devil will oppose you and even use people you know to try to discourage you but don't let that keep you from serving Jesus.

Your work for God is so important and no one else but you can reach the people God has for you to speak to. It's your calling, your work and God wants to bless you through it as well as others for His glory.

Encouraging one another even more as we see the Lord returning.

Look up for your redemption draweth nigh!

SEE YOU IN THE CLOUDS....................TO BE CONTINUE.

Jesus wore a stephanos crown made of thorns. He overcame sin,death & the devil for us and we have overcome this world all through our belief and trust in Him.

In a New Testament context, stephanos (or stefanos) is the Greek word for a victor's crown, wreath, or garland, symbolizing triumph in athletic games, contests, or military achievements, but also used metaphorically by Paul for Christian rewards like the "crown of righteousness" and the "crown of life". It differs from diadema, which referred to a royal band or fillet symbolizing kingly power.

 It symbolizes commendation, joy, and a perishable earthly prize contrasted with the imperishable heavenly rewards believers pursue. Unlike a kingly diadem, the stephanos is a victor's wreath, representing a reward for perseverance, faithfulness, winning souls, or faithful service, and may be called the crown of life, rejoicing, righteousness, glory, or incorruptibility.

A beautiful symbol that we will cast our crowns to the Lord.

Scripture reference for casting crowns in Revelation 4:10-11

King James Version

The four and twenty elders fall down before him that sat on the throne, and worship him that liveth for ever and ever, and cast their crowns before the throne, saying, Thou art worthy, O Lord, to receive glory and honour and power: for thou hast created all things, and for thy pleasure they are and were created.

Reassurance to use our talents God has given us.

Revelation 21:7 He that overcometh shall inherit all things; and I will be his God, and he shall be my son. He that hath an ear, let him hear what the Spirit saith unto the churches; To him that overcometh will I give to eat of the hidden manna, and will give him a white stone, and in the stone a new name written, which no man knoweth saving he that receiveth it.

THE 5 CROWNS

a. CROWN OF REJOICING

1 Thessalonians 2:19 KJV

For what is our hope, or joy, or crown of rejoicing? Are not even ye in the presence of our Lord Jesus Christ at his coming?

Luke 15:7

I say unto you, that likewise joy shall be in heaven over one sinner that repenteth, more than over ninety and nine just persons, which need no repentance.

b. CROWN OF RIGHTEOUSNESS

2 Timothy 4:8 KJV

Henceforth there is laid up for me a crown of righteousness, which the Lord, the righteous judge, shall give me at that day: and not to me only, but unto all them also that love his appearing.

Philippians 3:20 KJV

For our conversation is in heaven; from whence also we look for the Saviour, the Lord Jesus Christ:

c. IMPERISHABLE CROWN

1 Corinthians 9:24-25 KJV

 Know ye not that they which run in a race run all, but one receiveth the prize? So run, that ye may obtain.

And every man that striveth for the mastery is temperate in all things. Now they do it to obtain a corruptible crown; but we an incorruptible.

Matthew 6:19 KJV

Lay not up for yourselves treasures upon earth, where moth and rust doth corrupt, and where thieves break through and steal:

1 Peter 1:4 KJV To an inheritance incorruptible, and undefiled, and that fadeth not away, reserved in heaven for you,

crown of glory

Rejoicing

Ye have not chosen me, but I have chosen you, that you should go and bring forth fruit, and that your fruit should remain.

Incorruptible

Righteous

JOHN
CHIS VIG

crown of life

d. CROWN OF GLORY

1 Peter 5:4 KJV

And when the chief Shepherd shall appear, ye shall receive a crown of glory that fadeth not away.

Acts 7:55-56 KJV

But he, being full of the Holy Ghost, looked up steadfastly into heaven, and saw the glory of God, and Jesus standing on the right hand of God,

And said, Behold, I see the heavens opened, and the Son of man standing on the right hand of God.

Isaiah 42:8 KJV

I am the Lord: that is my name: and my glory will I not give to another, neither my praise to graven images.

Galatians 1:5 KJV

To whom be glory for ever and ever. Amen.

Romans 8:18 KJV

For I reckon that the sufferings of this present time are not worthy to be compared with the glory which shall be revealed in us.

e. CROWN OF LIFE

Revelation 2:10 KJV

Fear none of those things which thou shalt suffer: behold, the devil shall cast some of you into prison, that ye may be tried; and ye shall have tribulation ten days: be thou faithful unto death, and I will give thee a crown of life.

1 John 2:25 KJV

And this is the promise that he hath promised us, even eternal life.

James 1:12 KJV

"Blessed is the man that endureth temptation: for when he is tried, he shall receive the crown of life, which the Lord hath promised to them that love him."

SCRIPTURES FOR REFERENCE

ANXIETY

"Casting all your care upon him; for he careth for you." 1 Peter 5:7

"Be careful for nothing; but every thing by prayer and supplication with thanksgiving let your requests be made known unto God. And the peace of God, which passeth all understanding, shall keep your hearts and minds through Christ Jesus." Philippians 4: 6-7

"So that we may boldly say, The Lord is my helper, and I will not fear what man shall do unto me." Hebrews 13:6

"Peace I leave with you, my peace I give unto you: not as the world giveth, give I unto you. Let not your heart be troubled, neither let it be afraid." John 14:27

ASSURANCE

"Let us draw near with a true heart full assurance of faith, having our hearts sprinkled from an evil conscience, and our bodies washed with pure water." Hebrews 10:22

"He that believeth on the Son hath everlasting life: and he that believeth not the Son shall not see life; but the wrath of God abideth on him." John 3:36

"These things have I written unto you that believe on the name of the Son of God; that ye may know that ye have eternal life, and that ye may believe on the name of the Son of God." 1 John 5:13

"For our gospel came not unto you in word only, but also in power, and in the Holy Ghost, and in much assurance; as the know manner of men we were among you for your sake." 1 Thessalonians 1:5

"Verily, verily, I say into you, He that heareth my word, and believeth on him that sent me, hath everlasting life, and shall not come into condemnation; but is passed from death unto life." John 5:24

10 Fear thou not; for I am with thee: be not dismayed; for I am thy God: I will strengthen thee; yea, I will help thee; yea, I will uphold thee with the right hand of my righteousness.

BAPTISM

"There is one body, and one Spirit, even as ye are called in one hope of your calling; One Lord, one faith, one baptism, One God and father of all, who is above all, and through all, and in you all." Ephesians 4: 4-6

"Buried with him in baptism, wherein also ye are risen with him through the faith of the operation of God, who hath raised him from the dead." Colossians 2:12

"When John had first preached before his coming the baptism of repentance to all the people of Israel " Acts 13:24

"Then Peter said unto them, Repent, and be baptized every one of you in the name of Jesus Christ for the remission of sins, and ye shall receive the gift of the Holy Spirit." Acts 2:38

BRAVERY

"The wicked flee when no man pursueth: but the righteous are bold as a lion." Proverbs 28:1

"Finally, my brethren , be strong in the Lord, and in the power of his might." Ephesians 6:10

"And in nothing terrified by your adversaries: Which is to them and evident token of perdition, but to you of salvation, and that of God." Philippians 1:28

COURAGE

"Be of good courage, and he shall strengthen your heart, all ye that hope in the LORD." Psalms 31:24

"Wait on the LORD: be of good courage, and he shall strengthen thine heart: wait, I say, on the LORD." Psalms 27:14

Have not I commanded thee? Be strong and of a good courage; be not afraid, neither be thou dismayed: for the Lord thy God is with thee whithersoever thou goest. Joshua 1:9

Fear thou not; for I am with thee: be not dismayed; for I am thy God: I will strengthen thee; yea, I will help thee; yea, I will uphold thee with the right hand of my righteousness. Isaiah 41:10

DISCERNMENT

"But the natural man receiveth not the things of the Spirit of God: for they are foolishness unto him: neither can he know them, because they are spiritually discerned." Corinthians 2:14

"For the word of God is quick, and powerful, and sharper than any two-edged sword, piercing even to the dividing asunder of soul and spirit, and of the joints and marrow, and is a discerner of the thoughts and intents of the heart." Hebrews 4:12

Study to show thyself approved unto God, a workman who needeth not to be ashamed, rightly dividing the word of truth. 2 Timothy 2:15

"But strong meat belongeth to them that are of full age, even those who by reason of use have their senses exercised to discern both good and evil." Hebrews 5:14

DOCTRINE

"For I give you good doctrine, forsake ye not my law." Proverbs 4:2

"Preach the word; be instant in season, out of season; reprove, rebuke, exhort with all long-suffering and doctrine." 2 Timothy 4:2

"Jesus answered them, and said, My doctrine is not mine, but his that sent me." John 7:16

"Till I come, give attendance to reading, to exhortation, to doctrine." 1 Timothy 4:13

"For thou hast said, My doctrine is pure, and I am clean in thine eyes." Job 11:4

"Let the elders that rule we'll be counted worthy of double honour, especially they who labour in the word and doctrine." 1 Timothy 5:17

ENCOURAGE

"I can do all things through Christ which strengthen me." Philippians 4:13

"Cast thy burden upon the LORD, and he shall sustain thee: he shall never suffer the righteous to be moved." Psalms 55:22

"They encourage themselves in an evil matter: they commune of laying snares privily; they say, Who shall see them?" Psalm 64:5 (Some good and bad encouragement out there)

"wherefore comfort yourselves together, and edify one another, even as also ye do." 1 Thessalonians 5:11

"The LORD is my strength and my shield; my heart trusted in him, and I am helped: therefore my heart greatly rejoiceth; and my song will I praise him." Psalm 28:7

ENDURE

"But thou, O LORD, shalt endure for ever; and thy remembrance unto all generations. " Psalms 103:12

"But the LORD shall endure for ever: he hath prepared his throne for Judgement." Psalm 9:7

"Thou therefore endure hardness , as a good soldier of Jesus Christ." 2 Timothy 2:3

Wherefore seeing we also are compassed about with so great a cloud of witnesses, let us lay aside every weight, and the sin which doth so easily beset us, and let us run with patience the race that is set before us

Looking unto Jesus the author and finisher of our faith; who for the joy that was set before him endured the cross, despising the shame, and is set down at the right hand of the throne of God.

For consider him that endured such contradiction of sinners against himself, lest ye be wearied and faint in your minds. Hebrews 12 1-3 kjv

EVANGELISM

" But watch thou in all things, endure afflictions, do the work of an evangelist, make full proof of thy ministry." 2 Timothy 4:5

"And he gave some to be, apostles; and some, prophets; and some, evangelists; and some, pastors and teachers;" Ephesians 4:11

"And he said unto them, Go ye into all the world, and preach the gospel to every creature." Mark 16:15

And you will say in that day:

'Give thanks to the Lord,

Call upon his name,

Make known his deeds among the peoples,

Proclaim that his name is exalted.'. Isaiah 12:4

EVERLASTING & ETERNAL LIFE

"For the wages of sin is death; but the gift of God is eternal life through Jesus Christ our Lord." Romans 6:23

"My sheep hear my voice, and I know them, and they follow me: And I give unto them eternal life; and they shall never perish, neither shall any man pluck them out of my hand. John 10:27

"In hope of eternal life, which God, that cannot lie, promised before the world began;" Titus 1:2

"Verily, verily, I say unto you, He that believeth on me hath everlasting life." John 6:47

"For God so loved the world that He gave His only begotten Son that whosoever believes in Him shall NOT perish but have everlasting life. John 3:16

FAITH

"For by grace are ye saved through faith; and that not of yourselves: it is the gift of God:" Ephesians 2:8

"Let us hold fast the profession of our faith without wavering; for he is faithful that promised; " Hebrews 10:23

"**Hebrews 11:1** Now faith is the substance of things hoped for, the evidence of things not seen.

"For whatsoever is born of God overcometh the world: and this is the victory that overcometh the world, even our faith." 1 John 5:4

FAITHFULNESS

"But the Lord is faithful, who shall stablish you and keep you from evil." 2 Thessalonians 3:3

"If we confess our sins, he is faithful and just to forgive us our sins, and to cleanse us from all unrighteousness. " 1 John 1:9

"Faithful is he that calleth you, who also will do it." 1 Thessalonians 5:24

"God is faithful, by whom ye were called unto the fellowship of his Son Jesus Christ our Lord." 1 Corinthians 1:9

Thy mercy, O Lord, is in the heavens; and thy faithfulness reacheth unto the clouds. Psalm 36:5

It is of the Lord's mercies that we are not consumed, because his compassions fail not. They are new every morning: great is thy faithfulness lamentations 3 22-33

Know therefore that the Lord thy God, he is God, the faithful God, which keepeth covenant and mercy with them that love him and keep his commandments to a thousand generations; Deuteronomy 7:9

FELLOWSHIP

"And have no fellowship with the unfruitful works of darkness, but rather reprove them." Ephesians 5:11

"Be ye not unequally yoked together with unbelievers: for what fellowship hath righteousness with unrighteousness? And what communion hath light with darkness? 2 Corinthians 6:14

"And they continued steadfastly in the apostles' doctrine and fellowship, and in breaking of bread, and in prayers." Acts 2:42

"That which we have seen and heard declare we unto you, that ye also may have fellowship with us: and truly our fellowship is with the father, and with his Son Jesus Christ." 1 John 1-3

"For where two or three are gathered together in my name, there am I in the midst of them." Romans 16:17

FORGIVENESS

"For thou, Lord, art good, and ready to forgive; and plenteous in mercy unto all them that call upon thee." Psalm 86:5

"To whom ye forgive anything , I forgive also: for if I forgave anything, to whom I forgave it, for your sakes forgave I it in the person of Christ;" 2 Corinthians 2:10

And forgive us our debts, as we forgive our debtors Matthew 6:12

"Judge not, and ye shall not be judged: condemn not, and ye shall not be condemned: forgive, and ye shall be forgiven:" Luke 6:37

"And be ye kind one to another, tender hearted, forgiving one another, even as God for Christ's sake hath forgiven you." Ephesians 4:32

"Forbearing one another, and forgiving one another, if any man have a quarrel against any: even as Christ forgave you, so also do ye." Colossians 3:13

Jesus saith unto him, I say not unto thee, Until seven times: but, until seventy times seven. Matthew 18:22

GOSPEL

"But if our gospel be hid, it is hid to them that are lost:" 2 Corinthians 4:3

"For Christ sent me not to baptize, but to preach the gospel: not with wisdom of words, lest the cross of Christ should be made of no effect." 1 Corinthians 9:14

"For our gospel came not unto you in word only, but also in power, and in the Holy Ghost, and in much assurance ; as ye know what manner of men were among you for your sake." 1 Thessalonians 1:5

"Even so hath the Lord ordained that they which preach the gospel should live of the gospel." 1 Corinthians 1:17

"That I should be the minister of Jesus Christ to the Gentiles, ministering the gospel of God, that the offering up of the Gentiles might be acceptable, being sanctified by the Holy Ghost. "Romans 15:16

" But I would ye should understand, brethren, that the things which happened unto me have fallen out rather unto the furtherance of the gospel;" Philippians 1:12

HOLY

"I beseech you therefore, brethren, by the mercies of God, that ye present your bodies a living sacrifice, holy, acceptable unto God, which is your reasonable service." Romans 1:12

"If any man defile the temple of God, him shall God destroy; for the temple of God is holy, which temple ye are." 1 Corinthians 3:17

"Wherefore the law is holy, and the commandment holy, and just, and good." Romans 7:12

" In whom all the building fitly framed together groweth unto an holy temple in the Lord:" Ephesians 2:21

"In the body of his flesh through death, to present you holy and unblameable and unreproveable in his sight: " 1 Corinthians 2

And the four beasts had each of them six wings about him; and they were full of eyes within: and they rest not day and night, saying, Holy, holy, holy, Lord God Almighty, which was, and is, and is to come. Rev 4:8   81

HOPE

"Blessed is the man that trusteth in the LORD , and whose hope the LORD is." Jeremiah 17:7

"Be good courage, and he shall strengthen your heart, all ye that hope in the LORD." Psalms 31-24

"For thou art my hope, O Lord GOD: thou art my trust from my youth." Psalms 71:5

"Looking for the blessed hope, and the glorious appearing of the great God and our saviour Jesus Christ." Titus 2:3

"In hope of eternal of eternal life, which God, that cannot lie, promised before the world began;" Titus 1:2

IDOLATRY

"Thou shalt not make thee any graven image, or any likeness of any thing that is in heaven above, or that is in the earth beneath, or that is in the waters beneath the earth:" Deuteronomy 5:8

"Turn ye not unto idols, nor make to yourselves molten gods: I am the LORD your God." Leviticus 19:4

"little children keep yourselves from idols. Amen" 1 John 5:21

"For they themselves shew of us what manner of entering in we had unto you, and how ye turned to God from idols to serve the living and true God;" 1 Thessalonians 1:9

"Thou shalt not make unto thee any graven image, or any likeness of any thing that is in heaven above, or that is in the earth beneath, or that is in the water under the earth." Exodus 20:4

"That ye abstain from meats offered to idols, and from blood, and from things strangled, and from fornication: from which if ye keep yourselves, ye shall do well. Fare ye well." Acts 15:29

INFLUENCE

"Be not deceived: evil communications corrupt good manners." 1 Corinthians 15:33

"He that walketh with wise men shall be wise: but a companion of fools shall be destroyed." Proverbs 13:20

"Iron sharpeneth iron; so a man sharpeneth the countenance of his friend." Proverbs 27:17

"Let your light so shine before men, that they may see your good works, and glorify your father which is in heaven." Matthew 5:16

"And do not be conformed to this world: but be ye transformed by the renewing of your mind, that ye may prove what is that good, and acceptable, and perfect, will of God." Romans 12:2

INTERCEDE

"Likewise the Spirit also helpeth our infirmities: for we know not what we should pray for as we ought: but the Spirit itself maketh intercession for us with groanings which cannot be uttered." Romans 8:26

"Wherefore he is able also to save them to the uttermost that come unto God by him, seeing he ever liveth to make intercession for them." Hebrews 7:25

"Who is he that condemneth? It is Christ that died, yea rather, that is risen again, who is even at the right hand of God, who also maketh intercession for us." Romans 8:34

"For there is one God, and one mediator between God and men, the man Christ Jesus;"1 Timothy 2:5

"And he that searcheth the hearts knoweth what is the mind of the Spirit, because he maketh intercession for the saints according to the will of God." Romans 8:24

JOY

"Yet I will rejoice in the LORD, I will joy in the God of my salvation." Habakkuk 3:18

"Thou wilt shew me the path of life: in thy presence is fulness of joy; at thy right hand there are pleasures for evermore". **Psalm 16:11**

"Whom having not seen, ye love; in whom, though now ye see him not, yet believing, ye rejoice with joy unspeakable and full of glory: Receiving the end of your faith, even the salvation of your souls." 1 Peter 1:8

"Restore unto me the joy of thy salvation; and uphold me with thy free spirit." Psalm 51:12

"But let all those that put their trust in thee rejoice: let them ever shout for joy, because thou defendest them: let them also that love thy name be joyful in thee." Psalm 5:11

JUDGING

"Judge not according to the appearance, but judge righteous judgment." John 7:24

"Ye judge after the flesh; I judge no man.

And yet if I judge, my judgment is true: for I am not alone, but I and the Father that sent me." John 8:15-16

Do ye not know that the saints shall judge the world? And if the world shall be judged by you, are ye unworthy to judge the smallest matters?

"Know ye not that we shall judge angels? How much more things that pertain to this life?" 1 Corinthians 6:24

"For if we would judge ourselves, we should not be judged.

But when we are judged, we are chastened of the Lord, that we should not be condemned with the world." 1 Corinthians 11:31-32

KNOWLEDGE

"The fear of the Lord is the beginning of wisdom: and the knowledge of the holy is understanding." Proverbs 9:10

"Apply thine heart unto instruction, and thine ears to the words of knowledge." Proverbs 23:12

"The heart of the prudent getteth knowledge; and the ear of the wise seeketh knowledge." Proverbs 18:15

"He that hath knowledge spareth his words: and a man of understanding is of an excellent spirit." Proverbs 17:27

"My son, eat thou honey, because it is good; and the honeycomb, which is sweet to thy taste:

So shall the knowledge of wisdom be unto thy soul: when thou hast found it, then there shall be a reward, and thy expectation shall not be cut off." Proverbs 24 13-14

LOVE

John 3:16 "FOR GOD SO LOVED THE WORLD THAT HE GAVE HIS ONLY BEGOTTEN SON THAT WHOSOEVER BELIEVES IN HIM SHALL NOT PERISH BUT HAVE EVERLASTING LIFE."

"Let brotherly love continue." Hebrews 13:1

"But as it is written, Eye hath not seen, nor ear heard, neither have entered into the heart of man, the things which God hath prepared for them that love him." 1 Corinthians 2:9

"But God commendeth his love toward us, in that, while we were yet sinners, Christ died for us." Romans 5:8

Proverbs 8:17 "I love them that love me; and those that seek me early shall find me."

"And above all things have fervent charity among yourselves: for charity shall cover the multitude of sins." 1 Peter 4:8

"Herein is love, not that we loved God, but that he loved us, and sent his Son to be the propitiation for our sins." 1 John 4:10

MERCY

"For he shall have judgment without mercy, that hath shewed no mercy; and mercy rejoiceth against judgment." James 2:13

"But the mercy of the LORD is from everlasting to everlasting upon them that fear him, and his righteousness unto children's children; " Psalm 103:17

Matthew 5:7 "Blessed are the merciful: for they shall obtain mercy."

"Praise ye the LORD. O give thanks unto the LORD; for he is good: for his mercy endureth for ever" Psalm 106:1

Exodus 33:19 "And he said, I will make all my goodness pass before thee, and I will proclaim the name of the LORD before thee; and will be gracious to whom I will be gracious, and will shew mercy on whom I will shew mercy"

OBEDIENCE

Colossians 3:20 "Children, obey *your* parents in all things: for this is well pleasing unto the Lord"

And Samuel said, "Hath the Lord as great delight in burnt offerings and sacrifices as in obeying the voice of the Lord? Behold, to obey is better than sacrifice, and to hearken than the fat of rams." 1 Samuel 15:22

Acts 5:29 – But Peter and the apostles answered, "We must obey God rather than men.

1 John 5:3 – For this is the love of God, that we keep his commandments. And his commandments are not burdensome.

Isaiah 1:19 – If you are willing and obedient, you shall eat the good of the land; We demolish arguments and every pretension that sets itself up against the knowledge of God, and we take captive every thought to make it obedient to Christ. 2 Corinthians 10:5

Hebrews 13:17 obey them that have the rule over you, and submit yourselves: for they watch for your souls, as they that must give account, that they may do it with joy, and not with grief: for that is unprofitable for you.

PEACE

When a man's ways please the LORD, he maketh even his enemies to be at peace with him. Proverbs 16:7

 Now the Lord of peace himself give you peace always by all means. The Lord be with you all. 2 Thessalonians 3:16

Isaiah 57:21 There is no peace, saith my God, to the wicked.

"Peace I leave with you, my peace I give unto you: not as the world giveth, give I unto you. Let not your heart be troubled, neither let it be afraid." John 14:27

Galatians 5:22 "But the fruit of the Spirit is love, joy, peace, longsuffering, gentleness, goodness, faith,"

PERSECUTION

"Yea, and all that will live godly in Christ Jesus shall suffer persecution" 2 Timothy 3:12

"Yet hath he not root in himself, but dureth for a while: for when tribulation or persecution ariseth because of the word, by and by he is offended." Matthew 13:21

" As many as desire to make a fair shew in the flesh, they constrain you to be circumcised; only lest they should suffer persecution for the cross of Christ." Galatians 6:12

Galatians 5:11 "And I, brethren, if I yet preach circumcision, why do I yet suffer persecution? Then is the offence of the cross ceased."

"Bless them which persecute you: bless, and curse not." Romans 12:14

"Blessed are ye, when men shall revile you, and persecute you, and shall say all manner of evil against you falsely, for my sake." Matthew 5:11

John 15:20 "Remember the word that I said unto you, The servant is not greater than his lord. If they have persecuted me, they will also persecute you; if they have kept my saying, they will keep yours also."

PREACHING

"But hath in due times manifested his word through preaching, which is committed unto me according to the commandment of God our Saviour;" Titus 1:3

"And my speech and my preaching was not with enticing words of man's wisdom, but in demonstration of the Spirit and of power:" 1 Corinthians 2:4

1 Corinthians 1:18 "For the preaching of the cross is to them that perish foolishness; but unto us which are saved it is the power of God."

Acts 8:4 "Therefore they that were scattered abroad went every where preaching the word."

Acts 28:31 "Preaching the kingdom of God, and teaching those things which concern the Lord Jesus Christ, with all confidence, no man forbidding him."

PROPHESYING

"Despise not prophesying" 1 Thessalonians 5:20

"Again he said unto me, Prophesy upon these bones, and say unto them, O ye dry bones, hear the word of the Lord." Ezekiel 37:4

"Wherefore, brethren, covet to prophesy, and forbid not to speak with tongues." 1 Corinthians 14:39

1 Corinthians 14:31 "For ye may all prophesy one by one, that all may learn, and all may be comforted."

"And the spirit of the LORD will come upon thee, and thou shalt prophesy with them, and shalt be turned into another man." 1 Samuel 10:6

Acts 2:17 And it shall come to pass in the last days, saith God, I will pour out of my Spirit upon all flesh: and your sons and your daughters shall prophesy, and your young men shall see visions, and your old men shall dream dreams:

QUARRELS

"Do everything without grumbling or arguing," Philippians 2:14

Proverbs 15:1 "A gentle answer turns away wrath, But a harsh word stirs up anger."

Proverbs 15:18 "A hot-tempered person stirs up conflict, But the one who is patient calms a quarrel."

"Without wood a fire goes out; without a gossip a quarrel dies down." Proverbs 26:20

"From whence come wars and fightings among you? Come they not hence, even of your lusts that war in your members" James 4:1

Proverbs 17:14 "The beginning of strife is like letting out water, so quit before the quarrel breaks out".

"Have nothing to do with foolish, ignorant controversies; you know that they breed quarrels". 2 Timothy 2:23

REJOICING

"That your rejoicing may be more abundant in Jesus Christ for me by my coming to you again." Philippians 1:26

"But let every man prove his own work, and then shall he have rejoicing in himself alone, and not in another." Galatians 6:4

"For what is our hope, or joy, or crown of rejoicing? Are not even ye in the presence of our Lord Jesus Christ at his coming?" 1 Thessalonians 2:19

"Rejoicing in hope; patient in tribulation; continuing instant in prayer;" Romans 12:12

"Rejoice in the Lord alway: and again I say, Rejoice" Philippians 4:4

"But now ye rejoice in your boastings: all such rejoicing is evil" James 4:16

"I protest by your rejoicing which I have in Christ Jesus our Lord, I die daily" 1 Corinthians 15:31   "As sorrowful, yet alway rejoicing; as poor, yet making many rich; as having nothing, and yet possessing all things" 2 Corinthians 6:10

REPENTANCE

"Therefore leaving the principles of the doctrine of Christ, let us go on unto perfection; not laying again the foundation of repentance from dead works, and of faith toward God" Hebrews 6:1

"I say unto you, that likewise joy shall be in heaven over one sinner that repenteth, more than over ninety and nine just persons, which need no repentance." Luke 15:7

2 Peter 3:9 "The Lord is not slack concerning his promise, as some men count slackness; but is longsuffering to us-ward, not willing that any should perish, but that all should come to repentance"

Acts 5:31 "Him hath God exalted with his right hand to be a Prince and a Saviour, for to give repentance to Israel, and forgiveness of sins"

SEAL

"Nevertheless the foundation of God standeth sure, having this seal, The Lord knoweth them that are his. And, Let every one that nameth the name of Christ depart from iniquity." 2 Timothy 2:19

Revelation 10:4 "And when the seven thunders had uttered their voices, I was about to write: and I heard a voice from heaven saying unto me, Seal up those things which the seven thunders uttered, and write them not."

"And grieve not the holy Spirit of God, whereby ye are sealed unto the day of redemption "Ephesians 4.30

"Believers are said to be "sealed with the promised Holy Spirit," signifying their ownership by God and the assurance of their inheritance." Ephesians 1:13

"The Holy Spirit acts as a "seal" on believers, assuring them of their salvation and relationship with God." 2 Corinthians 1:22

SALVATION

" He only is my rock and my salvation; he is my defence; I shall not be greatly moved." Psalm 62:2

" For the grace of God that bringeth salvation hath appeared to all men" Titus 2:11

"Neither is there salvation in any other: for there is none other name under heaven given among men, whereby we must be saved." Acts 4:12

"Behold, God is my salvation; I will trust, and not be afraid: for the Lord Jehovah is my strength and my song; he also is become my salvation." Isaiah 12:2

Acts 28:28 "Be it known therefore unto you, that the salvation of God is sent unto the Gentiles, and that they will hear it."

"For God hath not appointed us to wrath, but to obtain salvation by our Lord Jesus Christ," 1 Thessalonians 5:9

SEEK

" But seek ye first the kingdom of God, and his righteousness; and all these things shall be added unto you." Matthew 6:33

"When thou saidst, Seek ye my face; my heart said unto thee, Thy face, Lord, will I seek." Psalm 27:8

" If ye then be risen with Christ, seek those things which are above, where Christ sitteth on the right hand of God." Colossians 3:1

Luke 19:10 " For the Son of man is come to seek and to save that which was lost"

"Seek ye the Lord, all ye meek of the earth, which have wrought his judgment; seek righteousness, seek meekness: it may be ye shall be hid in the day of the Lord's anger." Zephaniah 2:3

"Seek ye the Lord while he may be found, call ye upon him while he is near:" Isaiah 55:6

TESTIMONY

"Even as the testimony of Christ was confirmed in you:" 1 Corinthians 1:6

"And I fell at his feet to worship him. And he said unto me, See thou do it not: I am thy fellow servant, and of thy brethren that have the testimony of Jesus: worship God: for the testimony of Jesus is the spirit of prophecy." Revelation 19:1

"When he shall come to be glorified in his saints, and to be admired in all them that believe (because our testimony among you was believed) in that day." 2 Thessalonians 1:10

"And I, brethren, when I came to you, came not with excellency of speech or of wisdom, declaring unto you the testimony of God." 1 Corinthians 2:1

"And it shall turn to you for a testimony." Luke 21:13

"To the law and to the testimony: if they speak not according to this word, it is because there is no light in them." Isaiah 8:20

TRIBULATION/TRIALS

"My brethren, count it all joy when ye fall into divers temptations; " James 1:2

" Rejoicing in hope; patient in tribulation; continuing instant in prayer; " Romans 12:12

" The Lord shall fight for you, and ye shall hold your peace." Exodus 14:14

"Blessed is the man that endureth temptation: for when he is tried, he shall receive the crown of life, which the Lord hath promised to them that love him" James 1:12

" Be careful for nothing; but in every thing by prayer and supplication with thanksgiving let your requests be made known unto God. And the peace of God, which passeth all understanding, shall keep your hearts and minds through Christ Jesus." Philippians 4:6-7

2 Thessalonians 1:4 "So that we ourselves glory in you in the churches of God for your patience and faith in all your persecutions and tribulations that ye endure:"

TRUTH

"For we can do nothing against the truth, but for the truth." 2 Corinthians 13:8

"I have not written unto you because ye know not truth , but because ye know it, and that no lie is of the truth." John 2:21

"That I might make thee know the certainty of the words of truth; that thou mightiest answer the words of truth to them that send into thee?" proverbs 22:21

"For I rejoiced greatly, when the brethren came and testified of the truth that is in thee, even as thou walkest in the truth." 3 John 1:3

2 Corinthians 13:8 "For we can do nothing against the truth, but for the truth."

"Sanctify them through thy truth: thy word is truth." John 17:17

John 8:32 "And ye shall know the truth, and the truth shall make you free."

John 16:13 "Howbeit when he, the Spirit of truth, is come, he will guide you into all truth: for he shall not speak of himself; but whatsoever he shall hear, that shall he speak: and he will shew you things to come."

UBELIEF

"For what if some did not believe? shall their unbelief make the faith of God without effect?" Romans. 3:3

"Who was before a blasphemer, and a persecutor, and injurious: but I obtained mercy, because I did it ignorantly in unbelief." 1 Timothy 1:13

"And he did not many mighty works there because of their unbelief." Matthew 13:58

"And he marvelled because of their unbelief. And he went round about the villages, teaching." Mark 6:6

Mark 9:24 "And straightway the father of the child cried out, and said with tears, Lord, I believe; help thou mine unbelief"

VICTORY

"For whatsoever is born of God overcometh the world: and this is the victory that overcometh the world, even our faith." 1 John 5:4

"O death, where is thy sting? O grave, where is thy victory?

The sting of death is sin; and the strength of sin is the law.

But thanks be to God, which giveth us the victory through our Lord Jesus Christ.

O death, where is thy sting? O grave, where is thy victory?

The sting of death is sin; and the strength of sin is the law.

But thanks be to God, which giveth us the victory through our Lord Jesus Christ." 1 Corinthians 15:55-57

"He will swallow up death in victory; and the Lord God will wipe away tears from off all faces; and the rebuke of his people shall he take away from off all the earth: for the Lord hath spoken it." Isaiah 25:8

WISDOM

Proverbs 9:10 "The fear of the LORD is the beginning of wisdom: and the knowledge of the holy is understanding "

Proverbs 2:6 "For the Lord giveth wisdom: out of his mouth cometh knowledge and understanding."

"For the wisdom of this world is foolishness with God. For it is written, He taketh the wise in their own craftiness" 1 Corinthians 3:19

"But unto them which are called, both Jews and Greeks, Christ the power of God, and the wisdom of God" 1 Corinthians 1:24

Proverbs 3:13 "Happy is the man that findeth wisdom, and the man that getteth understanding"

WORK

"Comfort your hearts, and stablish you in every good word and work" 2 Thessalonians 2:17

"Study to shew thyself approved unto God, a workman that needeth not to be ashamed, rightly dividing the word of truth.* 2 Timothy2:15

"And if by grace, then is it no more of works: otherwise grace is no more grace. But if it be of works, then is it no more grace: otherwise work is no more work" Romans 11:6

2 Timothy 3:16-17 "All scripture is given by inspiration of God, and is profitable for doctrine, for reproof, for correction, for instruction in righteousness:

That the man of God may be perfect, thoroughly furnished unto all good works."

" And we know that all things work together for good to them that love God, to them who are the called according to his purpose." Romans 8:28

WORSHIP

"For we are the circumcision, which worship God in the spirit, and rejoice in Christ Jesus, and have no confidence in the flesh." Philippians 3:3

"Speaking to yourselves in psalms and hymns and spiritual songs, singing and making melody in your heart to the Lord;" Ephesians 5:19

"For the Lord is great, and greatly to be praised: he is to be feared above all gods." Psalm 96 4-5

"God is a Spirit: and they that worship him must worship him in spirit and in truth." John 4:24

"Saying, I will declare thy name unto my brethren, in the midst of the church will I sing praise unto thee" Hebrews 2:12

"O come, let us worship and bow down: let us kneel before the Lord our maker." Psalm 95:6

Romans 10:2 "For I bear them record that they have a zeal of God, but not according to knowledge."

"For I bear him record, that he hath a great zeal for you, and them that are in Laodicea, and them in Hierapolis." Colossians 4:13

"As many as I love, I rebuke and chasten: be zealous therefore, and repent." Revelation 3:19

Psalm 132:13: "For the LORD has chosen Zion; he has desired it for his dwelling place."

Hebrews 12:22: "But you have come to Mount Zion and to the city of the living God, the heavenly Jerusalem"

Quoting Isaiah 28:16, Peter refers to Christ as the cornerstone of Zion, saying, "For in Scripture it says: 'See, I lay a stone in Zion, a chosen and tested cornerstone, and the one who trusts in him will never be put to shame'". 1 Peter 2:6

"Zion will be redeemed with justice, her repentant ones with righteousness" Isaiah 1:27

Psalm 48:1-2:

"Great is the LORD and most worthy of praise, in the city of our God, his holy mountain. Beautiful in its loftiness, the joy of the whole earth, is Mount Zion, the city of the Great King

Romans 12:11 encourages believers to "not be slothful in zeal, be fervent in spirit, serve the Lord".

Isaiah 59:17 describes God's own zeal, saying He "put on garments of vengeance for clothing, and wrapped himself in zeal as a cloak" to act righteously for His people.

"Who gave himself for us, that he might redeem us from all iniquity, and purify unto himself a peculiar people, zealous of good works" Titus 2:14

1 Peter 2:6: Quotes Isaiah, describing Christ as the cornerstone in Zion.

Revelation 14:1: The Lamb stands on Mount Zion with 144,000 people.

The end....

Bibles that are falling apart are read by people that are aren't!

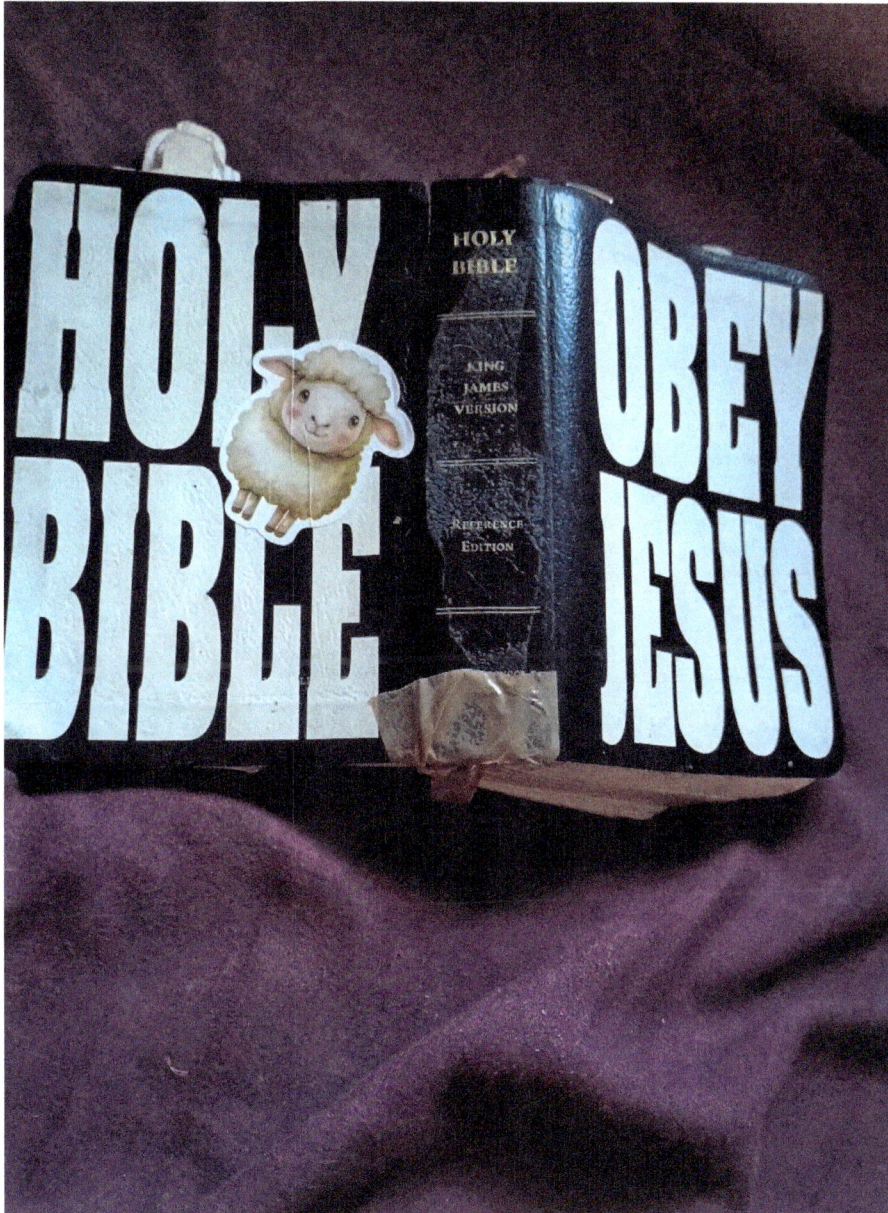

LOVE WARNS

Giving out motorbike tracts to people about driving safely and how to be saved

Printed in Dunstable, United Kingdom